PRAISE FOR

MW01228899

"A marvelously e~~~ ~~~~~~~~~~~~ ~~~~~~ ~~~~~~~~, a practical, spiritual self-help guide and a beautiful love story all rolled into one. Do yourself a favor and put this on your reading list. You'll find yourself reading it for the first time over and over again."

— *Regine Monestime, Black Butterfly Journeys*

"Inspirational Read! A compelling, honest story filled with challenges and triumphs. LaFonda Middleton gives you practical tools to move toward the happiness and peace you desire."

— *Audrey Wooten, M.D.*

"This book was truly a blessing. I could so relate. Thank you for being so supportive and for sharing your story."

— *Rebecca Davis, Founder/CEO, Restore Jacksonville*

"Awesome book! While reading, I was taken to so many places I've experienced in my life. I cried, laughed and re-evaluated my decisions ."

— *S. Gipson, Educator*

"LaFonda was so transparent and relatable. The tools are powerful – especially the forgiveness exercises. Great read!"

— *Twilla M., Educator*

"Of all the books I've ever read, this was by far one of my favorites. For me it was personal. It's almost like it was written just for me."

— Robin D. , Entrepreneur

"Very easy read. Very well written. I read the entire book in one night. It was a page-turner and very practical."

— Erica M.

"Having gone through a similar experience, and feeling the same guilt and shame as discussed in the book, it was comforting to hear someone I know personally who had go through a similar experience and was so transparent about it. A real person sharing real life situations and showing how faithful God is even when we aren't faithful to Him. This book is truly a testimony of how God will never leave nor forsake us. Thank you, LaFonda!"

—Tonya W.

"I connected with her story on so many levels and finished the book in one sitting! I highly recommend it to teenage girls and any mature woman still 'finding herself.'"

— Antionette J., Catastrophe Team Manager

FROM BROKENNESS TO HAPPINESS:
HOW I GOT OVER
AND
YOU CAN TOO!

LaFonda Middleton

ISBN: 9781726318334

Edited by: Marsha Malcolm and Amani Publishing, LLC
Author Makeup and Photograph: Renee Parenteau Photography
Hair: Iyana Sall
Cover Design By: Bogdan Matei

Scripture quotations marked NIV are taken from the Holy Bible, New International Version®, NIV®. Copyright © 1973, 1978, 1984, 2011 by Biblica, Inc.™ Used by permission of Zondervan. All rights reserved worldwide. www.zondervan.com The "NIV" and "New International Version" are trademarks registered in the United States Patent and Trademark Office by Biblica, Inc.™

Scripture quotations marked HCSB are taken from the Holman Christian Standard Bible®, Used by Permission HCSB ©1999,2000,2002,2003,2009 Holman Bible Publishers. Holman Christian Standard Bible®, Holman CSB®, and HCSB® are federally registered trademarks of Holman Bible Publishers.

Scripture quotations marked NLT are taken from the Holy Bible, New Living Translation, copyright ©1996, 2004, 2015 by Tyndale House Foundation. Used by permission of Tyndale House Publishers, Inc., Carol Stream, Illinois 60188. All rights reserved.

Scripture quotations marked ESV are from the ESV® Bible (The Holy Bible, English Standard Version®), copyright © 2001 by Crossway, a publishing ministry of Good News Publishers. Used by permission. All rights reserved.

Scripture quotations marked NKJV are from the New King James Version®. Copyright © 1982 by Thomas Nelson. Used by permission. All rights reserved.

Some scripture quotations are taken from THE MESSAGE, copyright © 1993, 1994, 1995, 1996, 2000, 2001, 2002 by Eugene H. Peterson. Used by permission of NavPress. All rights reserved. Represented by Tyndale House Publishers, Inc.

DEDICATION

This book is dedicated to my husband, Marshun Middleton. Thank you for loving me and putting up with my early morning hours writing this book.

To my sons Cameron and Jordan: dream big; the sky is the limit.

To my friend Regine Monestime for inspiring this book and motivating me to finish.

To my friend Audrey Wooten for pushing me beyond my limits. Iron sharpens iron. I appreciate you.

CONTENTS

ACKNOWLEDGMENTS

To my Lord and Savior Jesus Christ for leading and guiding me throughout the writing of this book. Thank you for gently nudging me during the times I grew weary.

To my husband, Marshun, for the love and support you have shown from the beginning of our relationship through the writing of this book and evermore. Your love and support helped me make it through this long and emotionally-draining journey. I love you.

To my boys, Cameron and Jordan, for loving Mommy unconditionally.

To my mom, Mattie, for always being my protector, my prayer warrior, my strength. Thank you for listening to every single chapter and offering no judgment but lots of love and support. You are my rock.

To my dad, Dave, thank you for loving and supporting me even when I tried to push you away.

To my sisters: Latrice, Michelle, and Felecia. I love you and thank you for your love and support. To Latrice: thank you for being one of my pre-readers and suggesting that I add notes pages and for always being willing to go to battle for me.

To my cousins: Tamalyn, Belinda, Kendal, Bre, and Aniesha, thank you for listening and encouraging me during our adventurous road trip to the Georgia mountains.

To my brother, Marquis, thank you for encouraging me to finish this book!

To my mother-in-law, Queen, thank you for your love and support and for showing and teaching your son how to love.

To my godmother, Doretha T. Haynes-Bodison, whenever we speak to or see each other, and no matter what I look like, you shower me with praise, compliments, love, and support. I love and appreciate you. Thank you for reading my script over and over again.

To my friends:

Regine Monestime, I know I'm going to mention your name several times, but it's only because you've played such an instrumental role in this project and in my life. Thank you for inspiring this book, for your encouraging words throughout this process, and for your Phenomenal Women Retreat in Mexico and your Gullah Retreat in South Carolina, where my thoughts were able to flow freely while I wrote and edited most of the book. Sometimes you just need to get away.

Audrey Wooten, thank you for reading my entire script, taking notes, making suggestions, and inspiring me to continue to work and improve this project, and then reading it again! You rolled up your sleeves and followed the prompting of the Spirit with your guidance and words of encouragement. Thank you for being a friend and showing yourself friendly.

Angela Cox, thank you for your love and support and for your honest assessment and review at the beginning of this project.

Hajoratu Iya, my first editor, thank you for the time and effort you put into my project and for your non-stop words of wisdom; for breaking bread with me; for your endless talks and text messages, and for always encouraging and inspiring me. I will forever be your "Learned Junior".

Syles Lewis for helping me fill in some of the blanks and for being as excited as I am about this project.

Richard and Leah Brown for helping me with some of the details and for your continued love and support.

Melina Buncome, Latasha Garrison, Detria Carter-Powell, thank you for taking the time to read part or all of my script despite your busy schedules.

Thank you to Denese Johnson for pestering me about the completion of this project because you know so many women will be blessed by it! Love you.

To my pastor, Russ Austin and his wife, Debbie Austin, thank you for meeting with me, encouraging me, and praying with me. Your support means the world to me.

To my former pastor, Bishop Rudolph Waldo McKissick,

Jr., thank you for your wisdom and encouragement through my second divorce and assistance with some of the details of this project. Your words have had a lasting impact.

To my book club sisters, Darlene, Leslie, Tiffany, Audrey, Mia, Benita, and Cheryl, thank you for supporting me, listening to the first reading, and offering your love and talents to make this project possible.

To the Black Butterfly Journeys Sisterhood of Phenomenal Women, Regine Monestime, Cece Cornelius, Stacy McClam, Redell Hearn, and Donna Mason, thank you for listening to the first few chapters, offering love and support, and allowing me space to write.

To my sisters from the Gullah Retreat with Black Butterfly Journeys, Regine Monestime, Donna Mason, Kaye Alexander, Elizabeth Galimore, Abigail Dunn, and Rochelle Lavenhouse, thank you for listening and offering your input and advice.

To Thamara Labrousse, I appreciate you pre-reading and offering suggestions on improving the script. Much love.

To Connie Clay, thank you for meeting with me and passing on lessons learned from your own books and sharing a wealth of information.

To my uncle Currey Gipson, thank you for being frank and candid with me as a young girl and now, during the writing of this book.

To my co-workers Jennifer Dickens and Julie Taylor, thank you for being a friend during those tough times and providing feedback for me during the writing of this book.

To Eric Terwilliger, your True North series helped to inspire this book. Thanks much.

To Dawn and Carter Wilson, thank you for your love and support. Carter, thank you for taking the time to read the entire script and offer your encouragement, suggestions, and continuous support.

To my pre-readers: Sherrine Gipson, Erica May, Robin Daniels, Rebecca Davis, Crystal Freed, Antionette Jackson, Twilla Mosley, Toni Gilliam-Harrison, Rebecca Davis, Tonya Wilcher, and Ida Mitchell - your feedback has been invaluable.

PREFACE

Before my thirtieth birthday, I was a two-time divorcee. I avoided discussing my marital history like the plague. I was embarrassed and ashamed, so I tried to re-write my story by avoiding conversations about it. Slowly, the Lord started to reveal to me that I was still in bondage to that part of my past. I was stifled by my own condemnation, shame, and fear of judgment. As a result, I began to open up about my past more and more. The more I talked about it, the more women approached me in private, thanked me for sharing, and shared their own stories. By sharing my own experiences, I was giving them a voice and freedom to speak.

A culmination of events occurred in 2016. On three separate occasions, I heard a variation of this phrase, "That thing that has caused you the most pain is the thing that

God wants to use." I'd heard this before, but it never resonated. In 2016, it resonated.

Pastor Eric Terwilliger taught a course at my church called "True North." This was one of the most amazing courses I have taken. In week five of the six-week course, he said, "God will take the hindrances in your life and not just heal them but use them as a channel of His love. You, in turn, will experience His love even greater." Well, I knew this to be true because I had already started to open up more about my past. Each time I shared my story and others shared with me, I could feel the move of the Spirit encouraging me to be open and vulnerable and also drawing me closer to Him.

As a result — with resistance, I might add — this book and opportunities to speak about my journey started to develop.

It is my hope and prayer that women and young girls will read my story and be encouraged by it, learn from my mistakes, and perhaps avoid some of the pitfalls I fell into face-forward.

You may read my story and start to feel sympathy for me. My pastor, Russ Austin, asked during one of his sermons when he was speaking of his past, that we not feel sorry for him, because sympathy would invalidate his past and all that he stands for today. Like Pastor Russ, my purpose for writing this book is not for you to feel sorry for me, but to tell my story in hopes that it will uplift, liberate, and free those who have suffered and/or continue to suffer.

At the end of each chapter, there is a 'Toolbox' of activities or suggestions designed to help you get over this hump in your life. If you complete the toolboxes, you will place yourself on the path of healing and wholeness. Allow me to travel through this journey with you. I look forward to seeing you on the other side where there is peace, freedom, and happiness.

CHAPTER 1
MY FIRST HEARTBREAK

For God has said, "But you are a chosen people, a royal priesthood, a holy nation, God's special possession, that you may declare the praises of him who called you out of darkness into his wonderful light."
1 Peter 2:9 (NIV)

When I was in the eighth grade, I had my life all figured out. I knew how it was going to evolve from beginning to end. I was going to marry my eighth-grade sweetheart — the love of my life, the apple of my eye. No one could convince me otherwise. Upon graduation from high school, we were going to get married; attend the same college; have two kids, a dog, a nice house with a white picket fence, and live happily ever after. The American dream. I had no doubt it would be mine.

You see, it was in the eighth grade that I gave in to his relentless pursuit, and I started "going with" my first boyfriend, Howell. He was my first long-term boyfriend, my first real kiss, my first everything. He worshiped and adored me, and I felt the same about him. We were inseparable. When we were not together, we were writing love letters to each other. Attending different classes created separation anxiety. We searched for each other during the few minutes between classes. He walked me home from school every day. We hung out every day after school. He came to visit me every Saturday and every Sunday after church. We lived about two blocks apart. During the first two years of dating, not one day passed that we didn't see each other. We dreamed about running away together.

In high school, he was the star basketball player and I was... well... his girlfriend. He was the point guard on the team. He could lead the team like no other. His athletic prowess was mesmerizing. He could shoot the ball from anywhere on the court and was especially adept at three-pointers. I attended every single home game and became one of the team scorekeepers just so I could attend the away games as well.

My life revolved around him. Sure, I engaged in other extra-curricular activities, including running track and serving on the executive board of the Student Government Association. But my life was so intertwined with his that I couldn't imagine an existence without him. We did homework together, we took long walks together, and we were forever connected in mind and spirit. We completed each other's sentences. We had the same core values. We were perfect together.

I remember one day, when he was visiting me at my grandparents' house. I had several cousins I'd grown up with, and we were very close in age. We were all within four to five years of each other. This evening, we had the music playing loudly and everyone was dancing, singing, and having a merry time. One of my cousins, Tam, took note of the fact that I was dancing off-beat. It was the funniest thing to her; however, it was quite embarrassing for me. So much so, that I stopped dancing and was ashamed because I had no idea what she was talking about. I thought you heard music and you just danced. I didn't realize there was a specific way to move to the beat.

That evening, while Howell and I were alone, we turned the music on, and he sat with me — patiently — and taught me how to find the rhythmic beat. When I finally got it, I was ecstatic. I had no idea that I had been dancing off-rhythm all that time. This happened when we were in the ninth grade. I was very much in love with him at this point.

He went on from there to teach me how to do simple dance steps to the beat. Now, I am still rhythmically challenged, but thanks to him, I can at least find the beat and move to it.

He was the one.

He was the one who would never hurt me. The one who would never betray me. The one who would never leave me. The one I could be open and vulnerable with. I would never have believed that he would be the one to take my heart and twist it in a wringer until it became unrecognizable. The one who would teach me what it means to be heartbroken.

Let me tell you a little more about Howell. He lied about simple things... things that did not matter. One of his first lies was about his middle name. Yes, he told me his middle name was one thing, and I found out years later that it was something completely different. He even wrote that fake middle name on the front cover of his school-issued books. He didn't like his middle name, I assume, but rather than just stating that, he made up an entirely new name and claimed it as his own. This was the first sign that he was a compulsive liar.

Another tale came a few months after our long courtship began. It was our first Valentine's Day together. Several days before, he told me he had purchased several gifts for me, including flowers, balloons, chocolate candy, and more. It was a young girl's dream. See, I had never had flowers, or candy, or cards, or anything else, delivered to me on Valentine's Day. I was excited, anxious, and happy to be acknowledged as someone's girlfriend and love on Valentine's Day.

A few days prior to Valentine's Day, I told my mom about his promised gifts. We were in the kitchen. I was sitting, and she was standing behind me, hot-combing my hair. She told me to be careful lest he not fulfill his promises. I thought that was nonsense. No one would say they had all these things for you if they did not, in fact, have them. It was still my eighth-grade year. On that Valentine's Day, I sat in my class, and I waited and waited for my name to be called. You see, all the students with Valentine's gifts were called over the intercom system to report to the main office to retrieve their gifts, and then they returned to class. My best friend, Rena, was called. She returned with roses and candy. I anxiously waited. My name was never called.

I thought maybe he had chosen to deliver my gifts in person instead of having them delivered at school. That was even more romantic than having my name called on the intercom. I waited all day for my flowers, my balloons, my chocolate candy, and everything else. They never came.

In fact, I would be 26 years old before I received my first flowers and Valentine's gifts. I was heartbroken. I don't even remember the lie he told about why he didn't get me anything for Valentine's Day. Though I can't remember his words, I vividly remember how heartbroken I felt. How embarrassed I was. I had told my mom and friends about all the items I expected to receive. I felt humiliated when the day ended, and I was as empty-handed as I had been when it had started.

His family was like mine. We weren't well-off by any means. We were poor — to put it mildly. Instead of admitting he didn't have any money to purchase gifts for me, he had lied. He could have made a

> *But you <u>could</u> end a relationship with someone for a pattern of dishonesty.*
>
>

homemade card with his heartfelt words — he was great with words. I would have been happy with that. As the alternative, he made up an elaborate story about all the things he had for me, and then he didn't deliver. He showed me who he was. I didn't believe him. Well, you would think that I would have learned not to fall for his lies again. I didn't.

Besides, you can't break up with someone because they didn't buy you a Valentine's Day gift, right? But you *could* end a relationship with someone for a pattern of dishonesty. I would learn this lesson much later in life.

Soon after the Great Valentine's Day Disappointment, Howell graduated from small tales that were forgivable to larger tales of unfaithfulness. Yes, there was a shift. The love of my life wanted to experience other loves. But I couldn't let go, didn't have the courage to. As a result, we continued on. He cheated, I forgave. He broke my heart, I forgave. He begged for forgiveness, and I said, "Okay, I'll forgive you, but please don't do that again, because the hurt was unbearable."

Stella, the first girl he cheated with, was a couple of years younger than us. We were in the eleventh grade then. There were a lot of rumors about him and this girl, but he vehemently denied them. I believed him.

One day, my best friend at the time, Cynthia, came to me and told me that she was at a house party with her boyfriend the previous night. There were a few other couples there. No adults were home. The lights were turned off. Slow music was playing, and they were all making out. She told me she saw Howell there with Stella. She said they were sitting in the recliner together, kissing and making out. This time, the information came from someone I trusted. My heart dropped. This was not how the story was supposed to go. I felt a stabbing sensation in my heart as it was pounding away.

It took all the courage I had to keep myself together

while speaking to her. I knew that, in fact, I had not seen Howell the night before and wasn't sure where he had been. In my heart, I knew it was true. I knew I had been betrayed. I didn't need him to confirm it. I confronted him with a tear-drenched face. I begged for answers while hoping and praying he would put my mind and heart at ease. He denied it. He said my friend was lying and was just jealous of what we had. He was very convincing. He assured me of his love for me.

I wanted desperately to believe him, but I couldn't, and we broke up. I had never cried so hard and so much as I did with that first break-up. All I wanted was to be alone. Alone in my pain and misery. Alone so I could pity myself as I listened to our songs. Alone to reminisce on all the good times we had shared and wonder how I was going to get along without him.

I missed him so much that it hurt physically. I didn't understand why he didn't miss me, too. After all, we had spent every day together for a couple of years or so and most days after that. Why didn't he try to talk to me? Why didn't he send me a message? Why didn't he call me?

And then I received the letter. The letter pouring his heart out. The letter confessing his undying love for me. The letter pleading to get back together with me. That letter made me blush like the school girl that I was. There it was, confirmation that he missed me, too. Confirmation that he loved me. Confirmation that he couldn't live without me. I was elated. I had won. Of course, I forgave him. Of course, I took him back. We were going to be together forever.

Things went along well for a while. We were happy again. After all, he saw that I would leave him if he acted up, so I was certain he wouldn't do that again. Unfortunately, my joy would be short-lived. The shenanigans continued. He would continue to cheat with the same girl. I would continue to forgive him.

I remember one morning before school, I was walking to the store with my Uncle Currey who is the same age as me. He told me as clear as he could that I should cut ties with Howell, who was also his friend. He said I deserved

> *I chose to ignore the writing on the wall, the verbal warnings given by friends and family, and the instinct I had deep down in my heart.*

better than the treatment I was getting. My uncle also told me he knew that Howell wasn't being faithful, but I wanted to believe things could be like they'd appeared to be before. Deep down I knew they couldn't. Alas, I chose to ignore the writing on the wall, the verbal warnings given by friends and family, and the instinct I had deep down in my heart. I continued on.

In our senior year of high school, Howell was offered an athletic scholarship to a nearby college. He also scored well enough on the ASVAB (Armed Services Vocational Aptitude Battery) Exam to enlist in the armed services and on May 3, 1989, he was extended an invitation to do so. I wasn't interested in the college he received the scholarship for, nor was I interested in him being miles away at a military base somewhere in or out of the country. He assured me that we would be together forever, that he had made mistakes, but I was the one for him. He even wrote it in my Senior Year Memories book. Here is a small excerpt of what he wrote:

> *Well. Check this out. I'm beginning my life with you all over again. I started off on the wrong foot in '89. That was a childish mistake. My love for you is stronger than that, and you know it as well as I do. I love you, Fonda, and I want you to know that nothing else is going to come between us. It's time for me to grow up and that's what I'm going to do because before you know it, we'll be out of school. Let's enjoy our senior year in school and look back at the good times we have shared together.* (He drew an arrow to a picture of us kissing).
>
> *College is ahead of you and the Army, or Navy, is ahead of me. There are going to be times like now, people trying to keep us apart, but it will never work. My plans are to marry you and make you happy at all times. I mean all the sorrows I've caused you will be made up, I guarantee that I love you, 'Shortkake.'*
>
> *Love 'H'*

I thought that was sweet. He wrote it in my senior book for all the girls to see. I was the chosen one. He declined his athletic scholarship and enlisted in the U.S. Army. After boot camp, he was stationed in Germany for two years. I lived at home with my parents and attended Albany State University. We wrote each other every day. E-V-E-R-Y DAY. There were always one or two letters in the mailbox when I came home from classes at the end of the day. It felt like our connection was getting stronger. Or was it?

Though we spoke on the phone often and put pen to paper every day, in college my eyes were finally opened to the endless possibilities. Oh my, the possibilities. In high school, Howell seemed larger than life, and I couldn't see anyone other than him. He took up the entire range of my vision. In college, I had a little distance and I could see.

My freshman year, I met a guy who made my heart turn flips. I denied these feelings and convinced myself that they would pass. We talked during and between classes, attended the same Bible study, and discussed many of our life's dreams and goals. I did not think it was possible that I could feel the same way about someone else as I did for Howell. But it was. There I was, flirty and giddy whenever I saw him. But when Howell came home during the holidays, he proposed as he had promised he would. And I accepted.

This was what I had been waiting for. Things were going according to plan. We set the wedding date for June 29, 1991.

I stopped flirting with my college friend and went full speed ahead with planning my wedding. Yep. The wedding was going to happen. Though Howell had already shown me who he was, I didn't believe him. I believed he had changed, and we would attain that American dream. I believed him when he said he loved me and would be faithful to me forevermore. I believed he had learned from his mistakes. I also believed I could deny my feelings for my college friend and move forward in a broken relationship.

Howell and I married at the ripe age of 20 years old. I remember the day like it was yesterday. I remember walking down the aisle wondering what in the world I was doing. My love for him was not in doubt. You see, a few months prior to the wedding, I had finally gotten up the nerve to talk to my mother.

I stood in the doorway of her bedroom and mustered up the courage to tell her I wasn't sure I was doing the right thing. My mother's sound advice was that I should follow my heart. I analyzed this statement. We had been tied together for six years, Howell and me. Of course I loved him. It was a no-brainer. I loved him and marrying him would be following my heart. Sure, I doubted his undying commitment to me. I doubted our connection. I knew it felt different. But I was at the point of no return. *Can't turn back now. Invitations have been mailed. Right?*

My mother and I continued to plan the wedding. We chose the reception menu items, confirmed the photographer and videographer, ordered bridesmaid dresses, and all the other necessities when planning a wedding.

On the day of our wedding, shortly before the ceremony, I was at my aunt Odessia's home across the street from the church, where I'd gotten dressed. I was all made up and waiting. Everyone gushed over what a beautiful bride I was. But on the inside, I was in turmoil. Was I making the right decision? I convinced myself it was just cold feet. Of course I was making the right decision. I was marrying the love of my life. I had been through so much with him; I had *earned* the right to marry him.

The time came for us to make our way to the church. I still had an uneasy feeling that I could not quell. I determined while walking down the aisle that this marriage was going to work. Though I knew I was making a mistake, we would be the epitome of a happily married couple. I would love, support, and encourage him. I would honor and obey him. Until death do us part. I resolved that we would be happy and eventually have that house with the white picket fence, two children, and a little dog running around. I was devoted to him.

On our wedding night, I cried. I cried because I knew I should have pulled the plug and walked away. I cried because it was too late. I cried because I had lacked the courage to be honest with myself. But I got myself together. After all, it was my wedding night.

After the wedding, we had a few days together in our hometown before he returned to his stationed base in Germany. He remained there until February 1992. I returned to college to complete my studies.

After his tour was over in Germany, he came home for a long visit right before Valentine's Day. We had a memorable visit. We spent a lot of time with our families and just connecting with one another. After Germany, he was stationed at Fort Hood in Killeen, Texas. I convinced myself that I was happy... *we* were happy. He promised me the moon and stars, and I expected him to deliver. Everything was well with us, or so I thought.

In 1992, I had an experience like I'd never had before in my life. I told you how connected we were despite his cheating ways. Well, in March, about nine months after our wedding, I was in my car driving back to campus after lunch. As I was driving and listening to my favorite CD, I was interrupted by a vision of Howell — having sex with someone else. I saw them both experience orgasms, their facial expressions were clear in my mind as they climaxed.

I know, crazy, right? I sure thought I was crazy. My imagination was running wild. Well, that night, I called him because I needed reassurance that everything was well with us. I needed to know that I was just hallucinating. On the call, he was very distant. He seemed to be overcome with guilt, but I didn't know if it was just my imagination or not. In my heart, I knew he had cheated on me. Of course, I didn't ask him if he had cheated on me earlier that day. I had nothing to base my suspicions on besides a "vision." I did what I was so proficient at doing — pretended all was well with us.

A few months later, in June, a couple of weeks before our first anniversary, I went to Texas to spend the summer with him. We had an apartment, and I'd planned to spend my days preparing for the Law School Admissions Test (LSAT) and my nights being a loving and doting wife.

One afternoon, a week after my arrival in Texas, Howell was off to work. It was a beautiful, sunny day. I decided to bake the peanut butter cookies that were in the kitchen cabinet. I started baking them. I was trying to muster up the energy to begin my studies, but it was such a nice day that I didn't. The aroma from the cookies was pleasing to my nostrils. I couldn't wait for Howell to get home. I was disrupted from my blissful moment when I heard a knock on the door. I was not expecting anyone and wasn't sure I should open the door since I was home alone. I decided I would. I opened the door.

A young woman, clearly upset, was at the door. I was certain she was the girl I had seen in my vision.

"Who are you?" she asked with attitude.

"I'm Fonda, Howell's wife," I responded, afraid to hear the answer to my next question. "Who are you?"

"I'm Karen, his girlfriend," she said. "I had been living with him until recently. He told me he had to move so I had to get my stuff out. Now I know why." She went on to describe our apartment and everything in it. She clearly had been in a relationship with him.

"How long have you been talking to him?" I interrogated.

"A few months," she said defensively.

"Where did you meet him?" I wanted to know.

"At work," she said.

I stood there in shock but determined to keep my composure. Oh, the hurt and devastation were indescribable. *Here we go again.* Here I was suppressing my feelings for my college friend and here he was, giving of himself to whomever. I had honestly thought the cheating was behind us.

I invited her in and we talked more. Karen was a simple, plain-looking girl. She was thin and stood about an inch or so taller than me. She had shoulder-length hair, a nice brown complexion, not much different from my own.

I learned that Karen was also enlisted in the Army. I wanted to be upset with her for messing around with a married man and all, but I quickly realized that it wasn't her fault.

First, she didn't know he was married.

And second, and more importantly, my issue was with Howell, not her. So, we talked. We compared notes. I'm not certain where the calm composure came from, because I was shattered inside. Perhaps God had already prepared me for what was to come in the vision I'd had several months prior to the visit. She was clearly hurt and upset.

She informed me that she had left a box of cookies in the pantry. By that point, the aroma of the peanut butter cookies was filling the tiny apartment. I asked her if she wanted some of her cookies, which were almost done baking by that point. She declined.

A short while later, Howell came home from work. He was wearing his Army fatigues. He pulled up with the music playing loudly — a Boyz II Men song. I could see him from the sliding glass doors that overlooked the parking lot. He couldn't see inside our apartment from the parking lot and was therefore clueless. He came inside, and that's when he saw Karen and me sitting there, waiting.

We both glared at him. He didn't know what to say or do. He asked her to step outside. I said, "No, you can speak to her right here."

He started to speak. I'm not sure what he said. Karen stepped outside. I stood in the doorway as well. They argued. She cursed and screamed at him and called him all kinds of no-good names. She was trying to strike him with her fists, but he kept blocking her blows. She threw a pair of his underwear at him; she had been carrying them in her purse.

Apparently, he had left them in her home. She also requested the key to her apartment. He took it off his keyring and gave it to her. I just stood in the doorway and watched in disbelief. It looked like a lover's quarrel. The only problem was, I was the wife. She stormed off a few minutes later in a rage.

When he stepped back inside, I took the glass I had been drinking from before she arrived and threw it in his direction. I couldn't remain calm any longer. The glass shattered against the wall, and I was sorry I'd missed him. I couldn't find anything else to throw. I tried to hit him with all the might I had, but he blocked my blows as well. My hands were trembling. My voice quivered as I demanded answers.

"How could you do this again?" I screamed.

In between strikes and sobs, he apologized. "I'm sorry, Fonda. I love you. It's not what you think. She's crazy." He cried and pleaded, then he cried and pleaded some more. His face was drenched with tears, his nose was running and red. He denied a relationship with Karen. Of course he denied it. It didn't matter that she had a pair of his underwear, and he had a key to her apartment.

He told me how much he loved me and how he couldn't live without me. That it was a big misunderstanding. He said they were friends. He and some other guys would hang out at her apartment after work and on weekends. He went on to explain that he must have had too much to drink one night and had to spend the night, and that's when he left the underwear. I thought, *But he doesn't drink.*

He said that she had also given him a key so that someone else would have a key to her place in the event of an emergency, and she also had his key. *I'm not sure why she knocked then.*

"Why was she so upset?" I asked.

"Because she was starting to like me, but the feeling wasn't mutual. She got upset when she saw you here." I wanted to believe him.

That weekend, he drove me home to Georgia. I was

officially done. I stayed home for a couple of weeks. We talked and talked on the phone. He tried unsuccessfully to convince me that Karen was lying on him. That she was out to get him and to destroy our relationship. That he was being set up. I didn't believe him, but I desperately wanted to.

He eventually confessed. He confirmed that the first time they were together was in March, confirming my "visual" experience. I decided that we were married now, and our marriage was worth fighting for. After all, he was contrite, apologetic, and willing to do whatever it took to make our marriage work. Consequently, I returned to Texas. We spent the summer trying to learn to love and trust again. It was a fragile time for us.

At the end of the summer, I returned to Albany State to finish up my senior year of college. I remember one day, I was sitting outside, speaking to my sister-in-law at my mother-in-law's home. She said, "Girl, you need to hurry up and move to Texas. Wives should be with their husbands."

In my heart, I knew she was right, but I also knew I wanted a career, and my education was a priority. Because in my other ear, I could hear my grandmother saying, after she learned that I was getting married, "Aw, hell! She ain't gone finish college now." She didn't know I'd overheard her speaking to someone else. For that reason, I accelerated my final college days by taking an overload of classes. I was determined to prove both wrong – after all, what did they know? A girl could have a marriage and a career too.

Though I still saw my male friend in college — we shared the same major — I was determined not to cross any lines. By the way, he now had a steady girlfriend, of whom I was jealous but had no right to be. Howell and I saw each other every chance we could. We continued to write each other and speak on the phone daily. We saw each other on all holidays and sometimes, he would surprise me by showing up for the weekend; however, evidence of his continued infidelity made it more and more difficult for me to ignore those feelings for my friend. Although I had desperately wanted them to, they hadn't miraculously disappeared after my wedding.

I accelerated what should have been some of the best days of my life — my college days. I made it through my senior year of college with ease and without incident. My college graduation occurred swiftly. I finished ahead of schedule, but took a few classes the last quarter since Howell and I decided it was best for me to stay at home with my parents in Georgia until he decided on re-enlisting.

In fact, my college days were far from over. I was preparing to attend law school. Howell chose not to re-enlist; therefore, the law school of my choice would determine where we would live for the next three years. It was an exciting time, because it would be the first time since being married that we were going to see each other daily. No more long-distance relationship. No more lies. No more infidelity.

Well, unfortunately, he was not done pursuing other relationships. When he returned to Georgia that summer, I was off participating in a summer program for entering law students at the University of Florida, and he was busy starting a relationship with one of our high school classmates. At this point, when the word reached me through a third party, I was not sure how to respond. We could *not* be going through this again. This time, when confronted, he admitted that he had failed me again. A silver lining: honesty.

Well, I thought, once we moved to Gainesville, away from all the temptation, we would be okay. We would start fresh. No temptations for either of us.

In August 1993, we moved to Gainesville so I could attend law school. He found a job, and I was busy adjusting to law school, my first real academic challenge. But all was not okay. After only a couple of months of school, I came home one day to find a Dear Jane note. Howell apologized to me for leaving so suddenly. He wrote in the letter that he had something to tell me, but he didn't know how. He inferred that someone was out to get him. Did I mention his elaborate lies? Well, this was not an exception. He took the car, leaving me without transportation. I called his mom and all his other friends and family that I thought he would call. No one knew where he was.

I remembered an old phone bill that had an unfamiliar Texas number that had been called frequently. Dissatisfied with his explanation at the time, I had saved the bill. Hence, when I received the Dear Jane note, I pulled out that old phone bill. Curious, I called that number. I learned from that phone call that it belonged to a young lady with whom he had been involved in Texas. This was not Karen, whom I had met earlier, but a different woman I had never heard of. A woman who had just delivered his baby.

Now, I thought I had experienced hurt before. I really did. I had become numb to the cheating. I convinced myself each time that we could get past it. Well, when I found out that this girl had a baby — *his* baby, his *first* baby — I was beyond devastated. She had now given him something I could never give him: his firstborn. This hurt was like no other. You see, we were no longer dealing with the act of infidelity in itself; this time, we were dealing with living, breathing evidence that would be with us for the rest of our lives.

The pain was so deep. I knew then that I could not save this relationship. I knew it was broken beyond repair.

He finally called late that night to explain why he had to leave so suddenly.

"Fonda, I had to leave to protect you," he said.

"What?!" I yelled, confused and upset.

"Let me explain."

> *The pain was so deep. I knew then that I could not save this relationship. I knew it was broken beyond repair.*
>
>

"Tell me why you left me here and why there's another woman that claims she just had your baby. Please tell me it's not true."

He went on to say that he'd donated his sperm to a sperm bank for extra cash. He later found out it was a corrupt organization, and this girl was part of the scheme. According to him, I was safer if he wasn't around for right now. He said the girl found out that he was the donor, and she had been stalking him. But because this was his sperm, he felt an obligation to care for the child. I told him to come home so we could work through this. He said he couldn't, because it just wasn't safe. "*They*" had found him.

Lord, help me. I desperately wanted to believe him, but his story made absolutely no sense, especially given the information I had already gathered prior to his call.

You see, just as I had done before, I spoke to the young lady, Dana. We had already compared notes. Our conversation was not at all friendly, but I learned what I needed to know. She claimed that he had promised to marry her and take her back to Georgia with him. They had even gone ring-shopping. Instead, he just up and left, never to return. She was several months pregnant at that time, and had been forced to have the baby alone. The baby was four days old the evening he left me. She had been searching for him and, in fact, had called every number she had until she'd finally located him in Florida. I felt sorry for her. We agreed to call each other when he called. Neither of us was sure where he was.

She eventually called me back after midnight that same night, and said he had called her. He was on his way to Texas to see her and the baby. Something in her tone was different, a gloating kind of *I won* tone. I thanked her for letting me know and asked her to never call me again.

I called his sisters to find out what they knew. It turned out I was the only one in the dark about this young lady. She had located his family weeks earlier. Apparently, they had been talking to him about "doing the right thing." Everyone had been having all these side conversations that affected my life and no one thought it was important enough to clue me in. I was the last to know. I felt betrayed by everyone who knew. That night, I stood in the shower and I cried. I cried and cried and cried. It felt as though my heart was literally crying tears of despair. The flow was uncontrollable.

I called my law school classmate, Syles. I knew she could pray me through this mess. She lived in the apartment complex across the street from ours. She came over around 3:00 a.m. with her pajamas on and a sleep bonnet on her head. Of course, she had been asleep. She sat with me. She talked to me. She prayed with me. She helped me make it through the night.

The next day at school, between classes, she saw me and the moment I saw her, I broke down again. I could not hold it together. I could not believe what was happening in my life.

You have twenty-four hours to get it together. Twenty-four hours to cry all you want to cry. After that, it's over. God did not bring you this far to leave you.

That day, Syles stood in the breezeway with me, cupped my face in her hands, looked down at me, and with a stern but loving tone, she said "Look at me. You have twenty-four hours to get it together. Twenty-four hours to cry all you want to cry. After that, it's over. God did not bring you this far to leave you. We have work to do."

I gave her the most incredulous look, thinking to myself, *What? Who gives a person twenty-four hours to grieve when they just found out their husband fathered a child with another woman?* But she was so matter-of-fact about it that I felt I had to comply with her command. Thus, I cried for a whole day. Any tears after that were silent and brief.

When I look back at that little girl who allowed herself to be continuously abused and mistreated, I want to hang my head in shame and sorrow. But I can't. If I do, you won't hear my story. I can't help you heal from your hurt. I won't get to give my testimony. So, I'll continue.

It hurts to admit it today, but I did the unthinkable. I took him back again. You see, when you are hurt and broken, you cling onto the familiar. When you think you can change a person, you allow yourself to accept all kinds of abuse. You can't walk away until you are sick and tired of being sick and tired. That being the case, I didn't walk away. I still wasn't ready. I could not imagine my life without him in it.

I absolutely did not want to be divorced. It was just not an option. As I saw it, my only choice was to hang in there and make it work. I knew we would have a tremendous testimony after all we had been through. Thus, I stuck with him. He changed his tune so many times about the baby that I didn't know what to believe. Sadly, I just wanted my marriage. I figured that one day, he would realize that I was the only girl that would put up with his foolishness and my willingness to forgive his transgressions would make him love and appreciate me even more. Of course, I was wrong.

He returned to Gainesville after a couple of weeks, but he was restless and unhappy. He decided that it would be best for him to return to our hometown and stay with his mom because he thought he could find a better job at home to support us. Plus, he said his mom was alone, sick, and needed him. A girl can't argue with that. A man who loves and cares for his mom. I knew he was full of stuff, but I wanted to keep the hope alive, so I stayed in Gainesville and struggled through my first semester of law school classes.

I went home on winter break not even certain if I would be allowed to go back to law school. I was certain that I had failed my classes. I'd never felt so unsure of myself in my entire life. So, while I was home, I spent time with Howell. I remember one night, we got a hotel room so we could have some privacy for the holidays. It was Christmas time, and all was merry and bright. As we lay in bed after making love, I could tell he was restless. I tried to assure him that we were on the right track. We were planning to return to Gainesville together after the holidays to give it another try, but I could feel him slipping away from me.

He rolled over and actually said to me, "She shouldn't be alone." *She* was Janet, the other hometown girl that I was certain was a short-lived fling and had gone away. To the contrary, Janet was worthy enough of his love and affection that he rolled over to his wife and pursed his lips to say that the girlfriend should not be alone during these holiday times. I suppose it was fine for *me* to be alone. I know I have already said a few times that the hurt he inflicted on me was immeasurable. Well, if there was icing on this miserable cake, that was it. I lay there in shock. I had lost him. So many questions ran through my mind. *Why is this happening to me?* I wondered. *Why am I not enough for him? Is she better in bed than me? Does he enjoy being with her more than he does me? Do they do some of the same things together that we do? Does he make her laugh? Does she make him laugh?*

The questions I was asking myself were torturous.

"Why are you doing this?" I finally silenced my racing thoughts long enough to ask him.

"I'm sorry, Fonda, I just can't do this anymore," he said.

"Why is she any different from all the others?" I asked.

"I don't know," he said. "I just know it's different with her. I feel different."

"But you're married! I'm your wife!" I screamed through

sobs. "Does marriage mean anything to you? What happened to being together forever?!"

"I'm sorry, I gotta go. I told her I would be there tonight," he said as he started to get dressed.

"Why the hell did you come here then? Why didn't you tell me this before having sex?" I asked.

"I was trying. I thought I could do it, but I can't." He walked out with no apparent remorse.

No matter how hard I tried to hang on to this man, he continued to pull away. He continued to inflict pain and despair. He did not want to be hung on to. I tried to figure out what was wrong with me. Guys flirted with me all the time. I thought, *I'm cute and a great catch. Smart girl, bright future. Why is this happening to me? What did I do wrong? Why am I not enough for him?* This feeling of worthlessness would plague me for years to come until I'd finally had enough; I finally gave up. I was broken.

Howell and I had started dating in 1985 at age 13. We married in 1991, when we were both 20 years old. We separated in 1993 at age 22 and divorced in 1995 at age 24. Often, I would wish for a re-do of those 11 years of my life, but in hindsight, I learned so much about myself, about relationships, about life. There's a silver lining in every story. I just had to find it. It took years, but I finally did. I will tell you how shortly.

TOOLBOX OF HOPE
TOOL 1: Pray Without Ceasing

In the book of Thessalonians, Paul advised the church in Thessalonica to rejoice always, and pray without ceasing. Like the Thessalonians, you must also pray often and constantly. If you are going through a divorce, have been through a divorce, have survived a toxic relationship, have been abandoned by a parent or parent figure... whatever your situation, you must pray for healing and deliverance.

When you pray, speak to God like you are having a conversation with a friend. He already knows your heart and your thoughts. Feel free to pour them out. Whatever you do, be intentional about your prayer life.

Include in your prayer praise to God for being a merciful, gracious, loving Father. Also remind Him of His many promises to His children. Be sure to include gratitude in your prayer. Be thankful for all He's done, even if you don't feel like expressing gratitude; there's always something to be grateful for.

Praying can be done in many ways. A few ways to pray without ceasing are:

1. Kneel and pray. There are many references in the Bible in which prayer was done while kneeling. Jesus knelt and prayed (see Luke

22:40-41 NIV). Kneeling shows deference, respect, and submission. You can kneel and pray at any time, but I suggest you kneel and pray when you wake up in the morning and before you turn in for the evening.

2. Walk and pray. You can take a prayer walk. With this form of prayer, you are simply taking a walk and during your walk, praying to God and expressing gratitude for His creations and all that He's done for you.

3. Drive and pray. While you are driving to work, running errands, or picking up your kids, turn the radio off and use this time to pray, meditate, and spend time with the Father, expressing gratitude or seeking assistance throughout your day.

4. Sing and pray. Play one of your favorite gospel tunes and sing and pray.

5. Clean and pray. Pray while cleaning your house, apartment, room, car, or workspace.

6. Sit in silence and pray. This is becoming one of my all-time favorites — to just sit quietly, not asking for anything or pouring my issues out, but sitting quietly and allowing God to speak.

A suggested prayer:

God, most merciful and loving Father. You are my Comforter in all afflictions. None can love me like You do. You are my protector and in You, I place my trust.

Father, You promised me in Your Word that You would heal the brokenhearted and that You would bind up their wounds. You promised in Your Word that Your mercies never end.

Father, I am standing before You today with a broken heart. I feel as though a part of me has been ripped away. Father, You know the pain, hurt, guilt, humiliation, and emptiness that I feel because of _____ (divorce, broken relationship, abandonment, etc.). Father, I know that this pain is temporary; however, it feels as though the agony will last forever. Please heal and liberate me from this constant feeling of loneliness, emptiness, shame, and guilt. Fill me up with Your love.

Father, I know that you are Jehovah El Shaddai, God Almighty. I come to You pleading, desperate, and asking that You liberate my soul. I come standing on Your promises to heal the brokenhearted. I believe Your Word. I thank You for the healing that is sure to come. Show me how to walk through this stage of my life. Help me learn the lessons You would have me learn, so that I can move forward. Thank

You for Your grace and mercy. Amen.

Lessons learned:

- ➤ You are worthy of love and affection.
- ➤ A relationship grows through continued acts of truth and honesty.
- ➤ You can't will a person to change. Change is between the person and God, but you don't have to suffer while they work through their process.

NOTES

NOTES

CHAPTER 2
WHY I STAYED

"Do not be afraid; you will not be put to shame. Do not fear disgrace; you will not be humiliated. You will forget the shame of your youth and remember no more the reproach of your widowhood."
Isaiah 54:4 (NIV)

In the days, months, weeks, and even years after our separation and subsequent divorce, I pondered why I had stayed. After a lot of reflection, journaling, and counseling, I realized there were a few reasons I'd stayed. Certainly, I loved him and would do almost anything to make it work. Also, I was very young and naïve when we courted and married. But it was more than that. I had to do a lot of soul-searching to find the answer.

First, I stayed because he validated the little, lost girl inside of me. He peppered me with sweet, romantic words, and not only did I believe them, but I clung to them for dear life. For example, in my Graduation Memories book, he wrote some of the lyrics to Regina Belle's song, "All I Want Is Forever," and wrote that he wanted to marry me and be with me forever. He wrote that he wasn't asking too much, just my love forever.

In actuality, forever *was* asking too much. He hadn't earned my love forever, but because I had a void in my life that I didn't know was empty until he showed up to fill it, there was no way I could return to the emptiness again. No way. When we were together, he made me feel warm and cozy inside. To him, I was worthy of love and affection. Don't we all want to be loved and validated? Doesn't every little girl want to be "Daddy's little girl"? I was no different. My daddy didn't show up to love on me until I was 17 years old. Instead of turning to God to fill that gap, I turned to Howell.

Whenever I was with Howell, I forgot about all the crap he'd put me through. Amazingly, I was able to numb all the pain when he was in my presence. But the moment he left my sight, just like a pain reliever that has run its course, all the pain came flooding back to me. It was a constant conflict of emotions. But the thrill of the emotional roller coaster ride far outweighed how awful I felt when we were apart. At least, that's what I thought.

I didn't know that God had already validated me. He had already counted me worthy. His hands were on me the entire time. He was always there. The void I was trying to fill in my own power and volition, God was there to fill freely, without pain and suffering. I just needed to be an open and willing vessel. Some lessons take longer to learn than others. It would be a while before I learned this one, but I finally did.

> *The void I was trying to fill in my own power and volition, God was there to fill freely, without pain and suffering.*
>
>

I also stayed because I loved what I thought we had — more than I loved myself. The beginning years of our six-year dating period were written right out of a fantasy book. At least, that's how I romanticized it. We were always together. We laughed and talked often. We both loved Jesus. I could share all my secrets with him.

For years, Howell was my safe place. We were so connected that he knew when it was time for my monthly cycle because he also experienced all the same symptoms - cravings, pimples on his face, everything. We were perfect together. When we began to disconnect, I refused to let go. I loved him with all the love I had to give, and I refused to envision a future without him. I was trying to hang on to and revive what had been. It was after that first couple of years, when it was so fabulous, that I should have walked away. I knew it was time, but I wasn't ready to let him go. I didn't have the courage to let go just yet.

I stayed because I was weak. Through my years with Howell, my self-confidence and self-esteem were washed away like sand on the beach during high tide — slowly and gradually. Soon the little girl, who was so full of life and confidence, started to disappear. I didn't recognize myself anymore. I behaved as if I was cowardly. I lost my voice and sense of worth. I didn't care. I just wanted him, whatever the cost. The longer I stayed, the more my self-esteem and confidence eroded, not to be seen for years to come. I was gripped by fear and self-doubt.

In reflection, I have now learned not to hang on to a situation longer than I'm supposed to. We were supposed to be together for a short period of time. Once we stayed in the situation longer than we needed, it started to crumble around us.

God was showing me, in little glimpses, life outside of Howell, but I was afraid to experience new things, and my fear caused me to cling onto the familiar. Sometimes, a person truly is meant to hold a space in your life for only a season. Howell taught me about love and how wonderful it could be. I should have gotten that lesson and moved on.

God said in His Word, *He has not given us a spirit of fear* (2 Timothy 1:7a). Despite my circumstances, He was there all along, equipping me. There was no reason for me to be afraid.

Another reason I stayed is that I was afraid of failing. I knew the stigma that came along with being a divorcee. I knew I would be judged. I knew this because I had judged. I was not willing to accept that as my fate. I didn't want people wondering what was wrong with me, wondering what I'd done to cause my marriage to fail. I had never failed at anything. I just hadn't. I was always the over-achiever. The idea of anything not working the way I'd planned was distressing to me. I couldn't bear the disappointment of my family. I was the one expected to excel at everything, including marriage. Anything I set my mind to, was accomplished. I had expected it to be the same with this relationship. If I set my mind to it, I would be able to make it work, and I desperately wanted it to work. Failure was not an option.

> *When I finally let go of the situation and let God handle it, I was liberated. I knew a freedom like I'd never felt.*

I finally learned to give it to God, to let Him be my strength. Relying on my own courage and power was a setup for an epic failure every time. When I finally let go of the situation and let God handle it, I was liberated. I knew a freedom like I'd never felt. The pain was deep, and I was certainly damaged goods. It was a process for me not to expect Howell's calls and his visits, and I missed our long talks. I didn't let go easily. I missed long talks with his mom and his sister — one of whom I was especially close with. It would take years to disconnect. But I finally did.

Today, I still love and adore his mom, who has now transitioned to glory. We spent many days sitting in her front room watching television and talking. That was a difficult relationship to sever, and it hurt both of us. She treated me like one of her own daughters. My picture, along with her kids, was in the front room where she spent most of her time. I didn't want to break up with her, but, in the only way she knew how, she forced us to break that bond. She forced me to move forward by telling me bluntly that her son didn't want me anymore, and I should stop coming around.

Now, at the time, I was crushed by her words and attitude toward me. I didn't realize that was her way of lovingly helping me to move forward and forget her son. Years later, as I write this, I'm overcome with emotions. Sometimes, those who love us must give us a 'tough love' kick in the shins to help us get unstuck. God sends angels in many forms. Accept the love kick, though it may be deathly frightening; the freedom on the other side is absolutely astounding.

TOOLBOX OF HOPE
TOOL 2: Memorize and Meditate on God's Word

Like David in the Bible, we must hide God's word in our hearts (Psalm 119:11). When feelings of hopelessness, desperation, sorrow, shame, and guilt start to creep up on us, consider meditating on God's Word before these feelings have an opportunity to take root. If we are feeling hopeless, let's go to the concordance of the Bible and it will guide us to Scriptures dealing with hopelessness. We may be feeling sad, depressed, lonely, or afraid. Whatever our emotions are, we can find Scriptures related to that emotion that speak to us and give us hope.

I found that reading God's Word and meditating on Scriptures helped to give me a sense of peace and calmness. Focusing on His word helped ease the anxiety and helplessness I was experiencing as a result of being rejected again and again. The anxiety of being thrown back into the dating pool, against my will, was overwhelming at times. I knew that He was going to work things out in my favor according to His Word, but sometimes I did doubt Him. During those times, it was important to meditate on Scriptures to keep me balanced.

A few suggested Scriptures for meditation:

➢ **Psalm 147:3 (NIV)** – "He heals the brokenhearted and binds up their wounds."

➢ **1 Peter 5:7 (HCSB)** – "Casting all your cares on Him because He cares for you."

➢ **2 Corinthians 5:7 (NIV)** – "For we live by faith and not by sight."

➢ **Lamentations 3:22 (HCSB)** – "Because of the Lord's faithful love we do not perish, for His mercies never end."

➢ **Matthew 6:34 (HCSB)** – "Therefore don't worry about tomorrow, because tomorrow will worry about itself. Each day has enough trouble of its own."

➢ **Isaiah 41:10 (HCSB)** – "Do not fear, for I am with you; do not be afraid, for I am your God. I will strengthen you; I will help you; I will hold on to you with my righteous right hand."

➢ **Isaiah 41:13 (THE MESSAGE)**– "That's right. Because I, your God, have a firm grip on you and I'm not letting go. I'm telling you, 'Don't panic. I'm right here to help you.'"

➢ **Psalm 56:8 (NLT)** – "You keep track of all my sorrows. You have collected all my tears in your bottle. You have recorded each one in your book."

➢ **Jeremiah 31:3 (NIV)** – "I have loved you with an

everlasting love; I have drawn you with unfailing kindness."

➤ **Isaiah 54:10 (HCSB)** – "'Though the mountains move and the hills shake, My love will not be removed from you and My covenant of peace will not be shaken,' says your compassionate Lord."

For the next week, please read, memorize, and meditate on a different Scripture each day. Choose from the list above or choose your own.

Then start to change your inner dialogue. For example, instead of "I am not loved," change it to "The Father said, 'I have loved you with an everlasting love'" (Jer. 31:3 NIV). Instead of "I am not worthy," change it to "For I am His workmanship, created in Christ Jesus for good works" (Eph. 2:10 ESV). Watch God transform your pain into a testimony for the edification of His Kingdom.

Lessons learned:

➤ The stories you tell yourself matter. You are worthy. You are loved.

➤ When it's time to let go, let go. Fear of failure will paralyze you if you allow it.

➤ Trust God.

NOTES

NOTES

NOTES

CHAPTER 3
MY RECKLESS BEHAVIOR

"Stay awake and pray, so that you won't enter into temptation. The spirit is willing, but the flesh is weak."
Matthew 26:41 (HCSB)

It was by the grace of God that I made it through my first year of law school. Academically, it was the worst of all my collegiate years. I'd always excelled academically despite my circumstances. The separation and subsequent divorce from Howell took a toll on me; however, I was happy that I'd survived my first year. I was determined to focus and make the next two years better than the first. Academically, they were. Socially, however, I was free as a bird. I hadn't been free since eighth grade. I didn't quite know what to do with myself. I was certain, however, that I was not going to be in a committed relationship for a while. I was not ready to open my heart to anyone just yet.

Consequently, I did the next best thing. After about a year, I became involved with someone who wasn't emotionally available to me. I did exactly what I had been a victim of for all those years. I got myself involved with Mike, a guy who was in a long-term, committed relationship. His girlfriend lived in another city while he was completing his college education.

I enjoyed my time with Mike. He was fun, intelligent, and most importantly, unavailable. It was perfect for me at that point in my life.

He would come to visit after classes and on weekends. We tried to be discreet about our secret rendezvous. I knew from the beginning that it wasn't a healthy relationship, but I thought I could handle it. We were honest with each other from the beginning. After all, I wasn't ready for love and just wanted to have fun. The fun included physical intimacy. I liked physical intimacy. I had no idea if or when I would marry again, and the idea of not being intimate at all was not appealing to me.

For me, the problem with exchanging bodily fluids is that my feelings *do* get involved. We started to like each other, but I knew from the beginning it was a dead-end relationship. He wanted me to ask him to leave his girlfriend, and I wanted him to reach the decision on his own.

However, even if he *had* made the decision, I wasn't certain I could ever fully trust him. I decided I was not going to be a coward this time around. I would end this relationship before I put too many years in. It was a difficult decision because I was enjoying myself, but I chose to break it off with Mike.

I broke it off, but he came back. Each time he came back, the spirit was willing, but my flesh was weak. I took him back time after time. I convinced myself each and every time that it was the last time. It happened that way over and over again. I enjoyed his company a lot and I especially enjoyed our intellectually stimulating conversations.

In the meantime, I had been attending a local church on a regular basis. My friend, Syles, who'd given me twenty-four hours to grieve my ex-husband, was a strong believer and she also had a positive influence on me.

One night, she and her best friend came over to my apartment for a slice of my deliciously famous strawberry cake. We sat and chatted for a bit and before I knew what was happening, they were praying for me and speaking in tongues. That night, I decided to rededicate my life to Christ and live His way. This meant that I had to end the toxic relationship with Mike. On the seventh attempt to break it off with him, I put my foot down and insisted that it was over.

I felt so pleased with my decision. I missed him, but I was really proud of myself. The courage that I lacked as a young girl, I had gained as a young woman. I was growing up and making bold and courageous decisions. I decided that I would be celibate. I decided to do things all the way God's way. I even joined the University Gospel Choir. I focused my energies on law school and studying the Word. I had never been happier with myself.

After about two months of celibacy and intense focus on the Word, I became ill. It was October 1995. I couldn't attend classes. I was feverish and sweaty. I felt nauseous and weak all over. I did what most young ladies would do in that situation, I called my mother. After I described my symptoms to her, she asked the question I hadn't even considered – "You're not pregnant, are you?"

With confidence, I replied, "No, I'm not." It had been over two months since I'd been sexually active. No way was I pregnant.

However, out of curiosity, I decided to purchase a home pregnancy test just to be sure. I returned to my apartment and took the test. The stick turned pink for "pregnant" within seconds. *Oh, no! How could this be? There's no way I'm pregnant!* I thought.

The shame and embarrassment engulfed me.

I was in complete shock and disbelief. The shame and embarrassment engulfed me.

Here I was, newly rededicated to Christ, and pregnant. There had to be a mistake, some cruel joke. It was my last year of law school. I was due to graduate on May 18, 1996. I quickly did the math and realized I would be as big as a house as I walked across the stage to receive my law school diploma. I would be responsible for a newborn while studying for the Bar exam. My life was over! My career was over before it started. Who would hire me at nine months pregnant on graduation day?

Worse yet, I was pregnant by a man who was not my husband and not available to me. So many thoughts went through my mind. *How in the world could I let this happen? What am I going to do? What is my mom going to say?*

I called Gail, another close friend and law school classmate, and we scheduled an appointment at the school's clinic for an official test. The official test confirmed that I was indeed pregnant. I was about nine weeks along.

I called Mike to tell him the news. He came over. He said he would support my decision, whatever my decision was. I just could not believe I went from being a married woman whose husband cheated and got someone else pregnant, to being the pregnant mistress. *Why now, after I've renewed my commitment to my God and Savior?* The irony was uncanny.

I decided that I would go against my beliefs and have an abortion. There was no way I could explain this pregnancy to my family. There was no way I could start my legal career off as a single mother. It just wasn't fair that I was two months celibate and now pregnant. I had to fix my bad decisions and I thought the only way to do that was to terminate the pregnancy.

Mike and I scheduled an appointment at the local clinic and went together. After completing the paperwork, I was escorted to a room, where I waited for the doctor. I cried so hard the doctor refused to perform the procedure. He sent me home to think about my decision. I was relieved. I only had a few weeks to make up my mind. The pressure was immense.

I went home and thought about it. Sadly, the next week, my fears got the better of me, and I decided once again to take a life that didn't belong to me. It happened on October 31, 1995. I was an emotional wreck. I have regretted that decision ever since.

After that ordeal, I was committed more than ever to letting God take the wheel. On my own, I was making a mess of things. I continued to remain celibate. Once I graduated from law school in May 1996, I moved to Jacksonville, Florida.

I decided that I really needed to work on my issues. I started reading self-help books and journaling. One book I read was called *Betrayal's Baby* by P. B. Wilson. It was a thought-provoking book about what betrayal will give birth to in our lives if we don't deal with the hurt and pain associated with it. In addition, I read *Knight in Shining Armor: Discovering Your Lifelong Love*, also written by P.B. Wilson. This was an engaging book that required a six-month commitment of not dating and focusing intently on preparing yourself physically, mentally, and emotionally in preparation for meeting Mr. Right.

I was about three months into my six-month commitment when I met the man determined to become my second husband.

TOOLBOX OF HOPE
TOOL 3: Forgive Yourself

Our sinful nature condemns us with guilt and shame. It is a fact that we all fall; we all sin. The problem arises when our dashed expectations of ourselves, and the expectations of others, cause us to retreat and our voices to be silenced as a result of our shame and humiliation. Remember, the enemy is the accuser of the brethren. He wants us in bondage.

Pastor Eric Terwilliger, now pastor of True North Church in Savannah, Georgia, stated it this way in a sermon series: "You don't have to wrestle with your flesh and your poor choices. Just walk in the love and grace of God."

Please know, God is not withholding His favor from you because you made poor choices. You will continue to make poor choices. Forgive yourself.

As I was writing this book, I was reading and sharing chapters with my mom along the way. This was the most difficult chapter for me to share, because I did not want her to lose respect for me. As I was reading aloud to her, I stole glimpses of her face. Her expression never changed. She smiled and nodded throughout the chapter. When I finished, she said, "Yes, I remember."

Huh? You remember? I thought. I was shocked.

Apparently, at some point in my brokenness, I had already shared my reckless behavior with her. I spent years in my own self-imposed prison for no reason. Shame and guilt will do that to you. She already knew. I was already free and didn't know it. Our heavenly Father is the same way. He already knows our dark secrets, yet He loves us anyway.

It is imperative that you forgive yourself. Forgive yourself for making poor choices. Forgive yourself for not following your instincts. Forgive yourself for not trusting God.

We have all made choices that we wish could be taken back; however, we must learn to accept our decisions and extend grace and courtesy to ourselves.

Pastor Eric said, "God will take the hindrances in your life, and not just heal them, but use them as a channel of His love." Imagine that, our darkest hour can be used as a vessel for God to demonstrate His love.

Freedom comes from forgiveness and telling our truths. God has taken our condemnation, sin, guilt, and shame, and He has already nailed it to the cross. We have to refuse condemnation. There is an amazing song by James Fortune and FIYA called "I Forgive Me." The beginning of the song is the statement, "Sometimes the hardest person for you to forgive is the one you see in the mirror every day. It's time for you to get free."

Priscilla Shirer writes in her book *Discerning the Voice of God, How to Recognize When God is Speaking*: "His goal is never to bring guilt and condemnation by continually reminding us about the sins of the past. Rather, He wants to bring healing and restoration by forgiving our sin and throwing it into the sea of His forgetfulness. God's desire is to lovingly lead us into His grace."

This statement is so true and so powerful. She goes on to say:

"So if the message you're hearing as you seek to discern His personal will and plan for your life is condemning or rooted in fear and intimidation, making you feel unworthy or incapable, then it isn't the voice of God who loves you. It is the voice of the Enemy, seeking to use your vulnerability to deceive you." (pp. 98-99)

As you work through your forgiveness process, I encourage you to recite the following affirmation:

The Lord has forgiven me, so:

- I forgive myself for imposing judgment on myself.
- I forgive myself for ignoring the inner voice of the Lord.
- I forgive myself for not trusting in my Father.
- I forgive myself for the poor choices I've made.
- I release myself totally of shame and guilt.
- Lord I accept and I thank You for Your

forgiveness.

Lessons learned:

> Self-forgiveness is imperative.
> Make bold and courageous choices, even when they hurt or you're afraid.
> Refuse condemnation.

NOTES

NOTES

NOTES

CHAPTER 4
IF AT FIRST YOU DON'T SUCCEED...

"I have said these things to you, that in Me you may have peace. In the world, you will have tribulation. But take heart; I have overcome the world."
John 16:33 (ESV)

As mentioned earlier, I moved to Jacksonville after taking the Georgia Bar Exam in July 1996. I had landed my dream job as an assistant public defender in Duval County, Florida. As a result, I took the Florida Bar Exam the following February. I started my legal career on August 5, 1996. As I mentioned, I'd decided that it was time for me to get myself together mentally, emotionally, and spiritually. It didn't take long to find my church home at Bethel Baptist Institutional Church.

I had made some unwise decisions and was ready to

get myself together. When I started reading *Knight in Shining Armor,* I had no plans of getting involved with anyone anytime soon. Therefore, I didn't think it would be a challenge to complete the author's six-month construction challenge. I was new to the city. I was studying for the Florida Bar Exam, and I was not interested in a new relationship.

I was about three months into my transformation process when Bethel had its annual singles banquet. It was a Friday night in late October, I believe. I had no plans that night, so I attended. There was lots of fun, games, music, and dancing. It was an enjoyable banquet. I had court hearings that Saturday morning, so I decided to leave early. As I headed out, I was stopped by a gentleman I hadn't met. His name was Tony and he was a member of the church. He offered to escort me to my car, and I graciously accepted.

Tony and I stood outside my car and talked for what seemed like hours. I thought he was cute, with a nice smile to boot. He was a breath of fresh air. We exchanged numbers. The next morning, while in bond hearings, I received a page from a number I didn't recognize (yes, a page). I was concerned that it was another attorney from the office paging to inform me of a defendant I needed to look out for while in court. Uncertain, I asked the judge for a brief recess so that I could respond to the page. I stepped outside the courtroom and returned the call. It was Tony, the gentleman I'd met the night before.

"Hi there," he said.

I was so shocked that I laughed. I was thrilled. I said, "Hi. I'm in court. Can I call you when I'm done?"

"Oh, I'm sorry about that," he said apologetically. "Yes, I'm looking forward to your call."

After court, I called him. We agreed to meet for a late lunch at a restaurant downtown near the courthouse. He was so easy to talk to. I learned more about him, including the fact that he was an associate minister at the church. He looked at me with such intensity; it was exciting and nerve-racking at the same time. It was as though he was looking right through me, reading my every thought. It was a pleasant day. I called my girlfriends, Leah and Regine, and told them all about my new friend.

That week, Tony and I spoke often on the phone. I told him about my six-month challenge and that I was only three months into it. He was very supportive. In fact, he offered to complete the remaining three months with me. Oh, he was promising — a man who loved Jesus as much as I did. He was also supportive and single with no children and no emotional baggage.

The next few days were filled with calls and meetings.

I started to feel a bit overwhelmed with his attentiveness and began to withdraw. He noticed the change immediately and asked me to call him if I wanted to chat. He said he didn't want to force himself on me. I felt awful that I had been called out. It appeared as though he knew me very well, though we had only met a few days before. He was very perceptive. I missed him right away and I called him before too long.

The following week, I invited Tony over to dinner to meet my close friends, Richard and Leah. We laughed, talked, and had a wonderful time. They seemed to get along well. Leah encouraged me to take it slow. I assured her I would. After all, I had three more months of my transformation journey and so I figured if God intended for this relationship to develop into more, I would know by the end of that time period.

A few days after our dinner with my friends, he wrote me the sweetest letter. I knew I was in trouble. A few excerpts from it are as follows:

> When I first noticed you that evening (referring to the night we met), I thought you looked very distinguished with your bright pretty smile, your beautiful complexion, and cheek-bones, and your warm soft eyes. Although I found you VERY BEAUTIFUL, it wasn't until I spoke with you the following day and saw a glimpse of your

heart and your strong value that you place on family, which struck me as a sweet, sincere, intense person, that I realized you are a very special young lady....

You are reassuring to me in so many ways because I can see GOD'S grace at work in your life, and it is good to see your desire for wisdom and understanding. Keep seeking and praying for it, and He will gladly reward you with more of His spirit. Although I have only known you for a short time, I can compare you with the thousands of believers that I have come across over my ten years since giving my life to Christ. I want the best for you and wish you much happiness and peace in your life as this chapter of your life unfolds greater experiences, greater love, and the rewards of your harvest....

I am falling for you, and I am not afraid of the feelings that I have for you; however, I am concerned with doing things right to avoid mistakes that would not complement our ideas about a relationship. I want you to know that I want you in my life, and I want to be an important part of your life. I want to be the most important person in your life, apart from God. I want you to be the person by my side to celebrate when I reach my hundredth birthday, greeting me with a kiss like you did when you first kissed me...

It went on and on.

Whoa! Wait. What? We just met. I wasn't sure about being by anyone's side for that long at that point in my life. I was still a wreck from the first failed marriage. Something

(God) told me to slow this ride down, but I loved the letter. I loved being wanted. I loved being celebrated. I loved being validated, so I ignored my inner voice and plowed forward.

Unfortunately, neither of us honored our commitment to continue the construction program. At some point, I suppose I decided the promises I'd made to myself and to God weren't worth keeping. Or I decided that he was worth breaking my promises for. Either way, the construction was not completed. I did insist on remaining celibate, however. He said he respected my wishes. I really didn't think it would be an issue for him anyway, considering he was a minister. We started spending more and more time together. Things were progressing swiftly.

An uneasy feeling overcame me, but I was uncertain why. The message was clear.

One day, we went to lunch at Miami Subs. He was standing, looking at the menu, and trying to decide what to order. I was standing behind him. An uneasy feeling overcame me, but I was uncertain why. The message was clear. My instincts were telling me to end this relationship and end it now. He had done absolutely nothing wrong, and I was certain I liked him a lot. Though I wasn't quick on the love talk, I enjoyed his company a great deal. I was silent on the way home. He noticed. He noticed everything. He was always so intense and perceptive.

"What's wrong?" he asked.

"Nothing," I lied. We continued to drive to my apartment in silence.

I soon brushed that feeling off and continued in the relationship, ignoring my instincts.

We grew closer and closer, and I was certain that I loved him. There were many nights when it was very difficult to honor my commitment to celibacy. There was lots of kissing and heavy petting. So much so, that some mornings, I woke up feeling like I'd dishonored God and my vow to celibacy before marriage. He would apologize and back off, but eventually, we ended up doing the heavy petting again. We were longing for physical intimacy. After one particularly steamy night, he wrote me a note apologizing for going too far. He ended with the following:

> *I feel and believe that if people do things within the guidelines of the Scripture, a lot of trouble can be avoided, and God's blessing will smile on their relationship because both people are seeking to do what's pleasing to Him. It's clear to me that you are at a place in your life that in all you do, you want it to be pleasing to God. I feel the same way, and I, for the first time, want to put my feelings*

aside to avoid compromising what we both want. You're not at the place you were in your life, emotionally and spiritually, that you were in when you dated your previous companions. I should be different because of what I know, which was not hard because everyone I dated before was not viewed with any future in mind. With you, I am looking at things with the present and future in mind, because I want your love and respect. I believe, to receive these, I must show myself respectable. I have waited a long time to experience love in its splendor, free of any fear or reservations, with someone I can grow with and share life with. If this is you, then I welcome the opportunity and hope that you can experience every part of love you've always wanted, freely, and equally. I find you very attractive and admit that I have a soft spot when it comes to resisting the urge to be held, caressed, just to share the simple intimacy apart from sex. I want you in my life, and I want you to want me also, and I want you to be free to want, not reluctant because of our physical wants. In hopes that you will be ready for a relationship, at some point now or later, I will limit being with you until you're ready, because I want your respect along with your love. I, most of all, want to do what's pleasing to Christ so that my heart and conscience can be clear and at peace.

That only lasted a day or two. We were drawn to each other like white on rice and longed to be in each other's presence; however, he did have one personality glitch that

FROM BROKENNESS TO HAPPINESS

was nerve-racking for me. He was ALWAYS so intense. Always analyzing everything I said and did.

The scary part is that he confessed to holding back with his intensity. He needed every thought and feeling fully developed. I couldn't just say I loved him, I had to explain why. As an attorney, I analyzed for a living, but to be analyzed all the time was exhausting and stressful. I thought I could deal with him and all of his deep, exploratory conversations. Communication is one of the main ingredients in any successful relationship, and he definitely believed in communicating. He was clear from the moment we met that I was a keeper, and that was enough for me.

That following Valentine's Day, he sent me the most beautiful bird of paradise floral arrangement. It was the first time in my life that I'd ever received flowers for Valentine's Day. Not only did I receive flowers, but he practically bought me a new wardrobe – eight outfits, which included dresses and suits. I loved every single outfit he bought. Amazingly, they were different sizes, but they all fitted perfectly. He had an eye for fashion and loved to shop. I, on the other hand, hated shopping. I could not believe my luck! I truly had hit the jackpot. That Valentine's was a stark difference from the one of my youth, when I'd had such anticipation, only to be disappointed. This one was sweeter. I had no expectations, since this was only our third month of courtship.

He was extremely attentive. I just knew I could handle his quirky habit of over-analyzing everything.

One day, after about a year of dating, he asked me to meet him for lunch at one of our favorite cafés, Judson's, now closed, in the Riverside area of Jacksonville. I was a little suspicious about this lunch, because earlier that morning he'd asked what I was wearing to work that day, which was unusual.

Judson's was a very small, quaint deli that served sandwiches, soups, and salads. There were about 10 or so small, square tables, each set for four. The tables were covered with fruit print tablecloths. We ordered our lunch and chatted while waiting on our food to arrive. After eating, he dropped on one knee right there in the restaurant. He was calm, confident, and in control.

"Fonda, I told you before, you are like no other woman I have ever met. I love you and I want to spend the rest of my life with you. I want to grow old with you. Will you marry me?" he asked.

I beamed, "Yes, of course I will marry you," I said.

He placed the most gorgeous ring on my finger. It wasn't the typical engagement ring. It contained several diamonds and was shaped like a budding flower. It was beautiful.

Our favorite waiter, Ron, came over and serenaded us with a song, the name of which escapes me. Applause broke out in the deli. We were congratulated and well wishes were shouted.

He was a girl's dream. He was attentive, supportive, and loving.

I went back to work elated. I told my supervisor and co-workers. "I's engaged now!" I announced, all giddy, while flashing my ring.

They were excited for me. My friends and co-workers, Jennifer and Julie, went straight into planning mode. "What's the date?" "Will it be in Jacksonville?" "Will you have a large church wedding or a destination wedding?"

"We haven't set the date and details yet, but you will be one of the first to know, I promise," I told them.

"I want to go dress shopping with you," said Jennifer.

"Of course," I said.

I called all of my friends and family. They were excited for me. My mom was thrilled. She liked Tony and was pleased with the upcoming nuptials. She was ready to start having grandbabies.

It was Tony's first marriage; he definitely wanted a wedding. We started planning right away. We decided to have a moderate-sized wedding at our church, Bethel

Baptist Institutional Church, in Jacksonville. We set the date for July 18, 1998.

During our engagement, I began to doubt that we were doing the right thing. He constantly pressured me to be intimate with him, justifying it by saying that we were going to get married anyway, and we didn't have to be super Christians. I kept reassuring him by responding that we didn't have much longer, and I was going to honor my commitment. I was disappointed that he didn't have enough self-control to hold out until the wedding. I was also disappointed that he was willing to break his vow to God. I wondered how strong his commitment would be to me if he couldn't fully honor God. I was determined to honor my commitment to remain celibate. It was only later that I would find out he didn't share my determination.

I continued to feel uneasy about going forward with the wedding. I thought maybe I was just a little nervous because my first marriage had been such a disaster. At that point, I thought the only issues I had with him were his extreme intensity, which I was certain I could handle, and his pressuring me to have sex, which would soon not be an issue as the wedding was fast approaching.

We sought pre-marital counseling through our senior pastor at the church, as well as professional counseling. During the counseling sessions with the professional, Tony expressed a number of concerns, including what he described as my lack of passion and desire for him. During one of the individual sessions, the counselor suggested to me that perhaps I was not the problem in our relationship. She tried to help me see that maybe we weren't a proper fit. I pondered her suggestion and decided to disregard it.

One day at work, I was speaking to Julie. She was in the middle of planning my bridal shower. She was asking me questions about the theme for the event. I confessed to her that I had some misgivings about getting married. She expressed concern and asked that I let her know before going forward with the shower. I said I would, but once I'd spoken the words aloud, I felt silly for questioning myself about marrying him. In hindsight, I wonder if my anxiety grew stronger around the same time he was dealing with his own issues. At any rate, we continued planning for the wedding.

Two weeks before the event, my right eye started itching and swelling like crazy. It appeared to be an allergic reaction to something. The whites of my eye were pink. Naturally, I thought it was Pink-Eye (conjunctivitis); however, Tony insisted that I was having a stress-induced allergic reaction to him. I assured him that was silly, laughable even. I went to the doctor and was prescribed drops for conjunctivitis.

After a few days, my eye was still itching and swelling and getting progressively worse. I went back to the doctor before the wedding. I had to get this cleared up before my big day. No way could I walk down the aisle with a swollen eye. It was immensely depressing. I felt quite unattractive and wanted to go in a dark room and hide until my eye returned to normal.

The day before the wedding, my eye was still huge, still itching, still swollen. Generally, the swelling would subside during the night, but I would wake in the morning to itching and by noon, it would be swollen again. The more I scratched it, the bigger it became. It itched so much that I felt that if I didn't scratch it, I would go crazy. I prayed so hard the night before to be spared the swelling on my wedding day.

On the morning of our nuptials, July 18, 1998, I woke up and my eye was a little pink but not very noticeable. It wasn't itching or swollen. I prayed all day. I was so happy there was no swelling. I walked down the aisle a little anxious that it would swell at any moment, but it didn't. I was happy and certain I was making the right decision.

The ceremony was phenomenal. Rudolph Waldo McKissick, Jr., our pastor, preached a sermonette. He spoke of an African story told by the griots in the village at weddings. He said the tale is, the ring finger is supposedly the only finger that has a blood vessel that goes straight to the heart. Once he said that, Tony's aunt caught the spirit and started shouting during the ceremony.

I thought, *Yes, this was the right decision.* I was certain, being a minister, Tony would never leave me. I was also certain that any issues we had would be worked through, especially given his communication skills.

Our reception was on a party boat called the Lady St. Johns. It was packed with 200 to 225 of our closest family and friends. When we entered the boat, music was playing, the dance floor was set up, and the food was ready to be served. We ate, drank, and danced. It was so much fun. I was happy I had no issues with my eye and thrilled we had survived the wedding day.

We'd made it through the day; and now, it was time for the big night. I was mentally and physically exhausted, but I was determined to deliver after having waited for eighteen months. That night we were intimate. It was a delightful night for us. We were finally able to fully express ourselves physically, with no guilt or shame.

The following Sunday morning, we left for our honeymoon, a five-day, four-night cruise to the Bahamas. That morning, my eye was itching and starting to swell yet again. Shortly after making it on the cruise ship, my eye was so swollen my eyelid was touching the rim of my sunglasses.

Eek! I wore sunglasses to hide it. It was embarrassing, unattractive, and unsexy. Ugh! I had already gone to the doctor twice in that two-week period prior to the wedding. I wanted to stay in bed and hide my face. My new husband convinced me to come out; after all, it was our honeymoon and our first cruise. We went out and explored the ship. He was anxious to return to the room to take advantage of me. The problem was that I didn't feel sexy at all, and the last thing I wanted was to be intimate. I felt like a freak, but I tried. He was disappointed with my efforts.

Monday morning, my right eye was well, but my left eye was swollen. It was worse than the right eye had been! *What in the world???* I went to the doctor aboard the ship. He prescribed different eye drops. My eye cleared up a little but not fully. Each morning, I awakened to a different swollen eye. They were alternating. I couldn't understand why three doctors couldn't figure out what was going on with my eyes. I had never suffered from any allergies. I hadn't eaten anything different. The only difference in my life was planning a wedding and getting married. Medically, it should have been simple to determine the origin and prescribe medication to remedy the problem.

Though I was having medical issues with my eyes I was still expected to perform in the bedroom. My communicative husband was very clear in expressing his disappointment with my performance. He expected that we would be swinging from the ceiling in the bedroom. So did I; it was just that I had big eyes that put a damper on my mood. I was praying and pleading for understanding. He had to know it would get better. He kept saying he was the one stressing me out and causing the reaction. Our cruise was five days and four nights. My eyes alternated swelling every one of those days.

When we returned home from the cruise, after less than one week of marriage, he had a major announcement.

"Fonda, after waiting all this time, I expected more," he said.

I nervously asked, "What are you talking about?"

"I expected you to be all over me on the cruise. It was anything but that," he said with anger and disgust.

"Tony, do you not see what's going on with my eyes? I'm sorry if I don't exactly feel sexy!" I exclaimed.

"You promised me that we would be doing it all the time. It's been five days and we've only been together a few times," he said.

"What? Really? Are you more concerned about sex than you are about my health?" I asked.

"No, but your eye doesn't stop other parts of your body from working," he said.

"No, it doesn't, but I don't feel attractive either. It will get better," I said softly.

"That's an excuse. I told you what I needed before we got married. If you knew you couldn't be what I needed, then you should have told me. If it doesn't get better in a year, there is no need for you to go with me when I leave for seminary school and no need to continue in this marriage," he stated, matter-of-factly.

I gasped in astonishment. He'd knocked the wind out of me. I could not believe what I had just heard.

"Are you serious?" I muttered.

"Yes, I'm serious. I refuse to be unhappy."

"Tony, we haven't even been married a week and you're already giving up on us?" I asked.

"I'm not giving up. I'm giving it one year," he said as he walked out the door.

I was completely undone.

I did what any self-respecting girl would do. I shut down and self-preservation kicked in. The walls went up and I was afraid to death to let them back down. *What in the world is wrong with me?*

I cried many silent tears into my pillow nightly.

My eyes continued to itch and swell. It started happening about every other week as opposed to every other day. I was happy for the break. I was thankful to get an appointment at the Mayo Clinic. There was a team of doctors evaluating me. A biopsy was conducted under my right eye. The biopsy results were negative. I underwent extensive allergy testing. Another negative. I was prescribed no less than 10 different eye drops over a period of time. None worked.

I refused to let my issues with my eyes interfere with my quality of life. Initially, I was calling into work, too embarrassed to show my face with big, swollen eyes. Instead, I started going to work despite my eye issues. I explained to my supervisor and the judges that I needed to wear sunglasses when my eyes were swollen. Everyone understood. The issue with my eyes was confusing to me.

Meanwhile, back at the ranch, I wasn't feeling too secure in my relationship. I expressed my concerns and my insecurities. On August 18, 1998, my husband of one month wrote me a note which included these lines:

> *I am promising to love you and only you for as long as there is breath in the both of our lungs. This is my commitment to you because you are a woman I love and because you are a woman I love, I will wait however long is needed for you to experience completed security in your soul. This is my hope because I have faith in my soul about God and His words are true. When fear, doubt, insecurities, and misunderstandings arise, I will remember God's promises and His love for us. This is my hope and my prayerful commitment to you.*

I wanted to keep the faith that our bond would only grow stronger after being tested so early on. But the fact was, I had been given a one-year deadline. I wasn't quite sure what to do with that. I tried to fight my way past the steel wall that had closed my heart shut. I lived in constant anxiety, wondering if I was going to survive a year. I needed this relationship to work. I rationalized that the only bone of contention was the frequency of our intimacy; I could work with that, once I got past the eye issues.

> *I tried to fight my way past the steel wall that had closed my heart shut.*

Our first New Year's night that we were together as a young married couple, about six months in, I was sick. I had flu-like symptoms and wanted nothing more than a hot toddy and my bed, but I knew there was no way we could bring New Year's in without being intimate. I mustered up all the strength I had, and I did it. It was a symbol that we would be intimate all year long and that I would survive the one-year deadline. All that mattered was making him happy and making this marriage work.

We carried on with day-to-day life for a while. Then one night, he disrupted the routine. He didn't come home, nor did he call. I had no idea where he was. Initially, I was angry, but the later it got, the more concerned I became. He had never stayed out all night before. I started calling every hospital in the city to inquire if he had been admitted. Nope, he was not in the hospital. I called the local jails. Nope, he was not in custody.

The following morning, he still had not returned. Worried, I called my friends, Richard and Leah, and explained the situation. They offered to help me search for him. They came over, but soon thereafter, he arrived home. He said he had driven to the beach to think and he'd fallen asleep in his car and lost track of time. Huh? Nothing about that story rung true to me. However, I did not think he was unfaithful to me because I believed him to be a man of his word. I thought he would leave me before betraying me that way, considering all I had been through. But I knew we had some serious issues.

That night, a non-drinking LaFonda drank an entire bottle of Arbor Mist wine. One glass after another. I tried to block out my pain and hurt, and that gnawing feeling inside me that he was being less than honest. I had no idea what a hangover felt like as I'd never drunk more than a glass or two of wine on special occasions. My mouth was dry. I felt dehydrated. I couldn't drink enough water. This was not me. Some changes had to occur in my life.

I could not bear the thought of being a two-time divorcee. I had done this relationship thing right this time, God's way. I was certain, after the wedding day, that I had made the right decision. I started reading self-help books about marital relations. His physical desire for me was much stronger than mine was for him. He needed to be touched every single day. Once or twice a week was plenty for me. The book helped for about a week, but then he got upset. He was angry because I had to read a book to help our lovemaking and my desire to jump his bones was not natural and daily. The agony.

Once again, I was barely hanging on to this relationship. My worst nightmare soon came true, when I came home one day after work and noticed his bags were packed and at the door.

"I think it's best for us to get a little separation for a while," he said.

"What does that mean Tony? Are you leaving me?" I asked.

"No, I just need some space." He said.

"Space for what?!" I yelled. "If you leave, it's the beginning of the end," I said.

"No, it doesn't have to be," he responded.

"Husbands and wives should live together and work through their issues. What happened to you doing all you can to make it work?" I wanted to know.

"I have been doing all I can. I don't see anything changing," he said.

I begged him to reconsider, but his mind was made up. He left.

We decided to try counseling with a different counselor. I *had* to make this marriage work. I still wanted my two kids, dog, and house with the white picket fence. He had promised me we would have that, together. I believed him.

We made several attempts to make it work. We had honest conversations, but he was mostly angry with me the majority of the time. He felt I had misled him about the anticipated frequency of our intimacy. I just didn't count on health issues that would make me feel like a freak. To him, it was just a convenient excuse.

During our separation, he started seeing other people. I found myself back where I was with my first husband, clinging onto hope as it slowly slipped through my fingers. I could not be divorced twice. The shame... the embarrassment... the humiliation. The thought of this caused me to dishonor myself. I knew the relationship was over, but I refused to be a two-time failure.

One night while I was still hopeful, I went to visit him at his apartment. His mom was there, and we were sitting in the front room talking when there was a knock at the door. *Déjà vu.* It was a woman. He stepped outside and spoke to her. She was loud and belligerent. Though he was clear that he was seeing other people, I'd never seen him with anyone else. He was respectful with it, if there could be such a thing. To be confronted with it helped reality to set in. He sent the woman away and came back inside. I wanted to relish in the thought that he'd chosen me. *But had he really?*

I finally decided that I was done. I was not going to devote another 11 years to a dead-end relationship. I accepted the fact that I would be a divorcee times two. Though it was a painful thought, in a way, I felt free. More liberated than I had felt in a very long time. I deserved to be happy in all aspects of my life, including my marriage. I was not going to be disrespected and dishonored.

> *I deserved to be happy in all aspects of my life, including my marriage. I was not going to be disrespected and dishonored.*

Two weeks after making the decision to let go, my eyes would swell for the very last time. As mysteriously as it had started two weeks before the wedding; mysteriously, it stopped two weeks after I gave myself permission to walk away.

TOOLBOX OF HOPE
TOOL 4: Seek Professional Counseling and a Supportive Inner Circle

I finally sought professional counseling after my second divorce, and it was one of the best gifts I could have given myself. I found myself looking forward to those weekly one-hour sessions. After each session, I felt lighter and more empowered.

Most medical experts will tell you one of the best ways to heal most open wounds is to keep it moist and allow the healthy skin cells to recreate. If you allow a scab to form too quickly, despite popular belief, it impedes the healing process. The scab creates a barrier, making it more challenging for healthy skin cells to form. The cells then must fight their way under the scab for the healing process to occur. However, if you take care to dress the wound properly and keep it moist, the healthy skin cells quickly form and heal the wound much faster.

Our minds and hearts are an open wound after a divorce or painful breakup. It is natural to want a quick and speedy recovery; however, healthy healing is the key. If you allow a scab to form, i.e., rebound relationships, heart-guarding (like I did), purposeful distractions like work or extracurricular activities, or any other 'coping' mechanism, it becomes more difficult for the healing to occur. Even then, the healing would have to fight its way through all the mess you have created.

Invest in your mental health by seeking professional counseling. Counseling offers an opportunity for you to be heard without emotions and without judgment. Often, just speaking about your situation helps to heal that open wound. Another major benefit to counseling is that coping tools are often given to help assist with the grieving process. Counseling can help you process your emotions.

You can help your healing process by seeking professional counseling to help you peel back the layers, truly heal, and free your heart to love again.

You can also seek local support groups. Often the cost for these groups is free or nominal.

We are not intended to go through life alone. Rather, we are to love and support each other in happy as well as tumultuous times. When Tony left, I really wanted to wallow in my depression all alone. I was too embarrassed and ashamed to call anyone. But I did. I picked up the phone and called my best friend, Regine. As soon as she said hello, I started bawling. I was able to tell her, between sobs, that Tony had moved out.

As a true friend does, she asked, "What? What did he do to you?" What did *he* do to *you*?

And then she asked, "Do you need me to come to Jacksonville for a visit?" I wanted her to, but I thought that was too much to ask. We both had full-time jobs. I remained silent and continued to sob in her ear.

A few days later, she drove from Miami and made herself available to me. The support was what I needed. We talked for hours on end, all times of the day and night, and I am so thankful. She made herself available to simply listen.

Of course, I also called my mom. Somehow, she always knew the right tone and the right words to say to me. She has played such a pivotal supporting role in my life. She has always been there to provide a listening ear and keep me focused on the Lord. After a visit or a phone call with her, my burdens somehow don't feel so heavy.

In addition, after making the decision to divorce, I reached out to my pastor at the time, Bishop Rudolph Waldo McKissick, Jr. He was at home recovering from minor surgery while I was going through hell. This was magnificent for me, because we emailed quite a bit. I cried out; he lifted me up, reassuring me of my worth and God's love for me. I kept those emails and, periodically, referred to them whenever I was going through a dark spell.

A support system has many benefits. A support system reassures you that you are not alone, offers you an outlet, and encourages you. From time to time, we all need to be lifted, encouraged, and loved.

Please do not go through this battle alone. If you don't have friends or family that you can call, find a local support group near you. You can call your local church or community center for guidance. But please, don't imprison yourself in the confines of your own mind. Eventually, you will explode if you don't give your pain and guilt an outlet.

Lessons learned:
- ➢ Trust your instincts.
- ➢ Listen to your body.
- ➢ Heal your wounds before moving to new relationships.

NOTES

NOTES

CHAPTER 5
TRUST YOUR INSTINCTS

"The eye is the lamp of the body. If your eyes are healthy, your whole body will be full of light. But if your eyes are unhealthy, your whole body will be full of darkness."
Matthew 6:22-23 (NIV)

In hindsight, I realize that I had disregarded my instincts. Tony and I just weren't a good fit. The level of stress and anxiety I felt with him was immense. I didn't realize how taxing the relationship was until it ended, and I experienced peace and serenity. God was whispering in my ears all along, but I couldn't hear Him because of all the other noise swimming around in my head, drowning His voice.

Though I had a relationship with God, it was selective. I trusted Him in some things but not all things. I wasn't close enough to Him that I could recognize His gentle whispers.

As a result of my refusal to see, my eyes were impacted two weeks before the wedding. I believe the mysterious problem with my eyes was a warning sign. I didn't see what was clearly before me. I am certain it was a sign because the problem stopped two weeks after I made the decision to stop fighting to maintain the relationship and give God total control. All I had to do was surrender.

It was clear that I still had not dealt with the emotional issues from my first marriage. At the time I married Tony, I was not ready for a serious committed relationship and certainly not another marriage. I had convinced myself that I was ready to move forward. I loved the institution of marriage and was ready to have babies. In my mind, I was supposed to have my two kids before I turned thirty. I found myself divorcing for a second time, six months before my thirtieth birthday. I had carefully planned my life, and it wasn't going anything like I had planned.

It was also clear, early in the relationship, that while standing in that Miami Subs restaurant, I'd had a premonition, a hunch, a feeling, an instinct from God to end the relationship because it wasn't right for me. I'd chosen to ignore that voice.

Sometimes, we make choices because they fit our agenda. Though I was saying I wanted to do things God's way, I didn't actually surrender everything to Him. God is not going to take our free will away. Our choices are ours to own. But He is right there to pick up the pieces.

He won't lead us wrong. His Word says, "'For I know the plans I have for you,' declares the Lord, 'plans to prosper you and not to harm you, plans to give you hope and a future.'" (Jer. 29:11, NIV)

We just have to trust Him. He knows the plan for us; we just have to follow the path. We may go straight or make a few detours along the way, but we must cultivate a relationship with Him, so His voice is loud and clear, and we know the direction He is leading.

> *"'For I know the plans I have for you,' declares the Lord, 'plans to prosper you and not to harm you, plans to give you hope and a future.'" (Jer. 29:11, NIV)*

It was clear that when Tony's faithfulness was wavering during our courtship — though I wouldn't know the level of unfaithfulness for a long time to come, God gave me the instinct, that gut feeling that told me to walk away — I heard the message but was searching for something tangible.

Oftentimes, we may not be able to explain why we need to take certain actions, but we have to learn to trust God and the instincts God has given us. It took two divorces for me to learn this difficult life lesson.

I struggled with the embarrassment of a second divorce. For years, I questioned my judgment. I questioned God and believed He had forsaken me. I questioned whether I would ever have that perfect love I'd heard songs about, read books about, seen movies about, heard stories about. I had been certain, as a young girl working in the fields of Georgia, that I would one day be in a loving and healthy relationship. I knew I would have a husband that loved and respected me. I had no doubt. Yet, here I was, divorced again. *Who will marry me now?*

I had to lift myself up, dust myself off, and try again. Or not.

TOOLBOX OF HOPE
TOOL 5: Trust Your Instincts

What does it mean to trust your instincts? To be led by the Holy Spirit? How do you do that? These are questions that many believers ask and are desperate for the answers to. At times, the prompting of the Spirit is loud and clear, it's at these times that we have developed an intimate relationship with Him.

After my second marriage ended and I was in the process of putting the pieces back together *again*, I met a gentleman while working out at the gym. He was tall, dark, and handsome with muscles bulging from everywhere. My my my. He approached me and introduced himself. We chatted while working out. He showed me a few weight-lifting tips. He was very charismatic.

He said all the right things, but my gut told me to be cautious. We exchanged numbers and during our first phone conversation we discovered that we were both friends with the family of a local judge who had recently passed. I was particularly close to this family. After we hung up, I called the judge's wife and asked her if she knew the gentleman because I had never seen him at any family functions. She paused, then told me to be careful. She suggested I speak to her daughter, who had more information about him.

After the conversation with her daughter and after conducting my own investigation, I learned he had a history of physical abuse towards women; he had cases pending for nonpayment of child support; the business he boasted about was closed, and on and on. Needless to say, I didn't call him back.

I am thankful that I chose to listen to those God-given instincts. I'm certain He saved me from more heartache.

When do you know the Holy Spirit is nudging you? I am still working on obedience in this area, but I will share with you what I've learned.

The Word of God says, "My sheep listen to My voice, I know them, and they follow Me" (John 10:27, NIV). We are His sheep and to know His voice, we must spend time praying, meditating, and communing with the Father. For me, His voice is not audible like a conversation with my mom. His voice is that inner gut, nudge, or instinct. It is not tied to a strong emotion. It is just a matter-of-fact, certain nudge that won't go away. It is gentle and more like a whisper in my ear. What He is prompting me to do or not do may not make sense to me at the time.

> *Feeling strong emotions about something or someone does not necessarily mean it is the will of God.*

The voice of God should not be confused with matters of the heart. Jeremiah said, "the heart is deceitful," (Jer. 17:9, NIV). Feeling strong emotions about something or someone does not necessarily mean it is the will of God. In discerning whether God is speaking to you consider the following:

1. God's voice is always consistent with the Word and the fruits of the Spirit. The fruits of the Spirit are love, joy, peace, forbearance, kindness, goodness, faithfulness, gentleness, and self-control (Gal. 5:22-23, NIV). Is the nudge you feel consistent with the Word? If not, that's not the Spirit. If so, it may be.

   Priscilla Shirer says in her book, *Discerning the Voice of God, How to Recognize When God is Speaking*: "He'll speak persistently. He'll speak personally. He'll speak with peace. He'll speak with challenge. And He'll roll it all together in the eternal counsel of His truth until His message echoes in your heart with heaven-sent authority. That's the voice of God." (p. 152)

2. Make an objective assessment of your body. Often, our sub-conscious is aware of danger before we are consciously aware of it. Do you feel the hairs on the back of your neck standing guard? Did your heart rate skip a beat unexpectedly? Do you have pause about a person or thing or idea but can't explain why? If you experience one or a number of these things, proceed with caution or don't proceed at all. You need to determine whether your own fear is holding you back or if the Spirit is warning you.

Take the time to pray to God for guidance in the situation. Be honest in your prayer and let God know that you are confused, but you know He's not the author of confusion. Ask Him to guide you on your next move. Then sit quietly, meditate, and wait for your answer.

3. Pay attention to events happening to and around you. In *Discerning the Voice of God*, Shirer writes, "persistent, internal inklings matched by external confirmation is often the way God directs believers into His will." (p. 82) Do you keep hearing the same message from different sources about a particular person, topic, or thing? That's what prompted me to write this book. Don't ignore all that is happening around you. Be conscious, alert, and aware of what's happening in your life.

4. Practice listening to your instincts. In your journal, write down when you have a nudge about something and document:
   a. How did it come to you?
   b. How do you feel?
   c. Any physical reactions in your body?
   d. Your actions – did you ignore it or respond to it?
   e. What subsequently happened?

This practice does not have to be a major life decision, but something simple.

For instance, I'm always searching for deals. A friend found this couch I was searching for to put in my boys' playroom. I was able to negotiate a great price for it. When the time came for me to pick it up, I hesitated. I have no idea why I hesitated, but I did. I decided to heed the warning and turn the deal down.

Was danger lurking? Perhaps. Is there a better deal for me? Maybe. Maybe not. I don't know yet, but I do know that couch wasn't for me. You may never know the answer to the why, but that's not important. What's important is to follow the prompting of the Spirit because He won't lead you wrong. Practice, practice, practice.

5 . There are many great books and articles on learning to hear the voice of God. One that I highly recommend is *Discerning the Voice of God: How to Recognize When God is Speaking* by Priscilla Shirer.

Lessons learned:
- Learn to listen to your instincts even when they don't make sense.
- God's voice is consistent with the fruits of the Spirit.
- The heart is deceitful and not to be trusted blindly.

NOTES

NOTES

NOTES

CHAPTER 6
UNDER CONSTRUCTION

*"Do not be conformed to this world, but be
transformed by the renewal of your mind, that by
testing you may discern what is the will of God, what
is good and acceptable and perfect."*
Romans 12:2 (ESV)

After my divorce from Tony was finalized, I started journaling again. My spirit was more broken than it was after the first divorce. After the first divorce, I thought, *Why me?* After the second one, I thought, *What's wrong with me?*

I found myself going back to P. B. Wilson's book, *Knight in Shining Armor.* It was a great starting point for me to get a grip on my emotional, spiritual, and physical life before I spiraled out of control. The pledge in the book read:

> Lord, I want you to fashion me for my prospective husband. I commit the next six months of my life for Your construction. I will surrender any area which is not controlled by You so that my life will bring You glory. (p. 15 Amazon Kindle version)

I made the commitment again and strengthened my resolve to follow it through this time. It would be one year before I seriously considered dating again.

One step in the book required me to reach out to those who had betrayed me and forgive them. I started with my father. My father had passed away right before I sat for the Georgia Bar Exam in 1996. I did not have a relationship with my father until I was 17 years old. Prior to that, I'd only seen him one time, in my seventh-grade year, as he was passing through my hometown.

In my tenth-grade year, I received a letter from my older brother, Pate, my dad's son, introducing himself. He included a picture of himself and my older sister, Felecia. I visited them a few times. After I turned 17, on one of my visits with them, my father came over to visit with me as well. I was happy to finally spend quality time with him. Once we finally connected, we remained that way until his death.

The last few months with my father were incredible. He had fallen ill and, thereafter, had a lot of free time on his hands. He called me every morning to say, "Good morning." He called me in the afternoon to see how my day was going. He called me at night to say, "Good night." He told me every chance he got that he loved me. After he passed, I really appreciated all of those calls and the outpouring of love in his last days.

However, I still needed to acknowledge that he'd abandoned me as a little girl when he wasn't there to guide me. I had to forgive him for not choosing me. I had to forgive him for not sacrificing for me. I had to forgive him for not demonstrating for me how a man should treat and love a woman. I had to forgive him for depriving me of being "Daddy's little girl." I had to forgive him for all the birthdays, Christmases, Father's Days, honor's programs, and graduations that he never showed up for. I had to forgive him for not walking me down the aisle. I had to forgive him for not filling that void that I chose to fill with men who would not honor and respect me. I had to forgive him for not teaching me about love.

One day, while sitting in my office, in the midst of this forgiveness process, I called my Uncle Red, my dad's brother. Since my dad had passed on, I wanted to speak to someone whom he was close with before he'd died.

That day as I spoke to Uncle Red, I was sitting in the conference room and I was overcome with emotion. At times, I could barely speak; I was weeping uncontrollably. I wasn't sure where all the emotions were coming from, since I thought I was already healed in that area. The forgiveness process was emotionally draining.

When I got myself together, I explained that I had questions about my dad and wondered why he'd been absent during my childhood. He assured me that my father had spoken of me often and wanted to spend more time with me. This was my first time hearing that he'd even spoken of me before we connected at age 17.

"We only lived an hour away from each other," I said. "Why didn't he just get in the car and come to see me?"

"It wasn't that simple for him," he said, "but I tell you what, I will be here for you from now on, since he's gone," he assured me.

I was 30 years old, but I cried like a five-year-old. I needed to free myself from that emotional baggage. The conversation with Uncle Red helped me take another step closer to emotional freedom. I had to re-write the narrative I had created about my father and his absence.

It would be remiss of me if I didn't note here that my stepfather came into my life when I was in the fifth grade. He did the best he could with me. I was well into adulthood before I truly accepted his love and support. I pushed him away at every turn because he wasn't my biological father, and I was afraid he was taking my mother from me. I thank God that, though he didn't know how to break past my tough exterior, he never gave up. God had given me what I needed, but I rejected it time and time again. You see, I wanted my "real" daddy. Today, I am grateful that my stepfather is loving and supportive of me and we have a fantastic relationship.

I also had to forgive Howell. I journaled a lot and completed a number of forgiveness exercises to help me through the process. I was angry with him for many years. I was angry because I'd given him my unconditional, unadulterated, pure love, and he hadn't appreciated it. I was angry because I had been completely open and vulnerable with him, and he'd treated my love with reckless abandonment. I had to forgive him for all the betrayals. I had to forgive him for all the lies. I had to forgive him for breaking our vows. I had to forgive him.

I had to forgive myself for not loving myself enough to walk away from Howell earlier than I did. I had to forgive myself for attempting to fill a void that only my heavenly Father could fill. I had to forgive myself for disregarding my instincts. I had to forgive myself for my lack of courage.

Finally, I had to forgive Tony, my second husband. He, being the formidable communicator that he is, agreed to meet with me and be open and transparent. Even with the writing of this book, he has made himself available and assisted with some of the details I had forgotten. We had several frank and honest conversations. For that, I am very grateful.

During one of the first conversations with Tony, while sitting on the couch at my house, he told me about his unfaithfulness while we were dating. Years later, I connected all the dots. My judgment was so clouded that I missed what was happening before my eyes. I was honestly shocked when I learned that he had one transgression during our courtship. He had slept with someone shortly before our wedding. And then, upon further reflection, I remember the conversation with my co-worker Julie as she was planning my bridal shower and the uneasy feeling I had but didn't know why. It must have been around that time that he was unfaithful. Instincts are such a powerful source if we just tap into them.

He also admitted to one other indiscretion during our marriage. It was the night he didn't come home. I had suspected, but I had convinced myself, at the time, that he would never betray me that way.

On one occasion, he met me at the beach and allowed me to complete an exercise that started with, "I forgive you for...." It was a useful exercise that helped me move another step toward healing. We sat on the beach facing each other.

He allowed me to speak my truth and offer my forgiveness. I forgave him for abandoning me. I forgave him for breaking his promise that we would grow old together. I forgave him for not giving us a chance. I forgave him for treating me like I was dispensable. I forgave him for not fighting for us, for me. I forgave him for making me a two-time divorcee. I forgave him for forcing me back into the dating pool.

I asked him to forgive me for marrying him although I knew I was under construction and not ready. I asked him to forgive me for shutting down once he told me he was only giving us a year before re-assessing whether to go forward with our marriage.

The forgiveness process was only the beginning of my construction. The author recommended journaling, memorizing Scriptures to help overcome the betrayal, taking care of my physical appearance, and reading several other suggested self-help books. This time, I completed the six-month construction period. Afterwards, I was still not ready to seriously date. I felt pretty confident that I had done my work and had adequately worked through my baggage, but I was not prepared to open my heart again.

Fast forward to May 25, 2002. Regine and I boarded the ship for the Tom Joyner Fantastic Voyage Party with a Purpose Cruise. We had our outfits ready for each day of the cruise. We were excited and ready for the time of our lives. Life was grand. I was content.

The next day, we signed up for the small group session with Iyanla Vanzant. We were fans of Iyanla's and had read several of her books and completed some of her workbooks. When we went to sign up, the session was already filled to capacity. We were told to be prepared to attend in the event participants did not show up on time. We were first in the "wait" line. Thank God, we made it in! Surprisingly, the group was very small, no more than around 25 women.

When we entered the room, we were immediately nervous. We asked ourselves, *What have we gotten ourselves into?* The description on the schedule was very vague. We had no idea what to expect. We remembered how blunt and straight-forward Iyanla was and is. But it was too late. The door was closed, and we did not feel free to leave. To make matters worse, we were told we could not sit next to someone we knew. We were seated in chairs that were positioned in an oval shape. Iyanla was sitting at the head. I was seated in the third position from Iyanla. My bestie was about halfway around the circle. We could not use each other as a crutch. Eek! There were several workers in the room standing behind us waiting to assist if needed. We were given a bottle of water and asked to be seated. The lights were dim.

Iyanla started by introducing herself and explaining the

rules. We could not speak of anyone else's experiences in the room. We could discuss our own as much as we wanted. She talked to us briefly and asked each of us to be prepared to complete a statement. I cannot remember the exact beginning of the statement, but it was along the lines of, "I forgive myself for...."

The two women that went before me were broken. Iyanla took her time with them and helped them to process through their pain. Soon, it was my turn. I was so frightened I wasn't sure what I was going to say or how much I wanted to share. I immediately crossed my legs and clasped my hands together tightly. She asked me to uncross my hands and legs and breathe. I needed to allow oxygen to circulate freely and allow my thoughts to flow freely. She said when I clasp my hands and cross my body parts, I am attempting to protect myself and not allow myself to be open and vulnerable. Iyanla said it also restricted the flow of blood and oxygen and, therefore, the flow of words and thoughts.

I thought she was exactly right, protect myself was just what I wanted to do; however, I obeyed her orders. I placed my hands in my lap and planted both feet on the ground. This simple act caused me to feel so open and vulnerable. I could not speak. I started to cry one of those ugly, difficult-to-breathe cries. She asked me to breathe and take as much time as I needed.

I took a few breaths. After several moments, I was finally able to speak. I started. "I forgive myself for making bad decisions in choosing husbands."

Iyanla stopped me, and said, "Forgive yourself because you knew before getting married, *you knew*." I sobbed uncontrollably.

The idea that I was not a victim of someone else's disrespect of me, but that I was my own problem, was a difficult pill for me to swallow. It was then that I really understood and accepted the fact that both times I knew I was making mistakes. I had to

> *The idea that I was not a victim of someone else's disrespect of me, but that I was my own problem, was a difficult pill for me to swallow.*

forgive myself for knowing and going forward with the marriages anyway. I wept. She allowed me to cry; she helped me process my emotions. She said we could stay as long as was necessary. Iyanla was going to sit right there with me in my pain until I was ready to release it.

The mood in the room was overwhelmingly heavy yet loving and supportive. I could feel the energy in the space. I could feel the women rallying around me as I struggled through my process. When Iyanla finished with me, I was an emotional wreck. I cried throughout the entire session while others spoke – it lasted for hours.

I had entered that room with a heaviness that I didn't know I had. I thought I had done my work and was ready to enjoy life without the excess baggage. I didn't know until after the session with Iyanla that I still had healing to do. I had to truly forgive myself. As I exited that room, I felt 10 times lighter than I had felt in years. This experience on the second day of the cruise helped lead to one of the best vacations that I have had in my life. The chains were broken!

After the cruise and my newfound liberation, I knew it was time for me to make space for the man God had been preparing for me all along. I was a bit gun shy, however. The fact was, I had been abandoned by my father and that abandonment had repeated itself two more times in my failed marriages. I was now certain that healing had occurred. I was not certain that I was ready to open myself up again. It took several months for me to get to the point of seriously considering dating anyone.

I read another self-help book, the name of which I cannot recall. The author suggested that all loose ends with previous relationships and current relationships be severed. Obediently, one day, I picked up my phone and made several calls to guys I had been involved with in the past. And guys I knew were interested in me in the present, but with whom I was being very vague and unclear about my intentions. I made it clear to them that I was unavailable to them from that point forward. After the calls, I felt much better. Freer.

Interestingly enough, though Howell and I are from a small town, and he was still living there, I very rarely saw him when I went home to visit, nor did I try.

A few months after my phone calls to other guys in my past, one of my uncles died, and I went home for the funeral. The service was on June 7, 2003. After the funeral, Howell stopped by my family's house to pay his respects and offer his condolences. It was our opportunity to talk. We went outside and talked for a while. He asked me to forgive him for all his transgressions. I was a bit taken aback at the apology and honesty. I apologized to him, as well. It was the closure I needed to close that chapter in my life. We were free to move forward, shackles of the past released.

The very next week, I met the love of my life, my husband.

TOOLBOX OF HOPE
TOOL 6: Forgive Those Who Betrayed or Abandoned You

I was blessed that both of my ex-husbands allowed me to express my feelings and give me the closure that I needed to move forward in my life. Not everyone will have the benefit of speaking directly to the person that hurt them; however, if the source of your pain is willing to sit with you, I encourage you to schedule a time where the two of you can speak freely without interruption. One exercise I suggest is similar to one I completed.

First, find a quiet environment. I recommend a neutral place with no memories attached to it. It can be at a park, a beach, a coffee shop, or restaurant with a quiet area to talk. Complete these two phrases:

"I forgive you for…."

"Please forgive me for…."

Complete each phrase as many times as necessary until you have exhausted all that you are forgiving for and all that you are requesting forgiveness for.

It is very easy to check off the laundry list of wrongs that have been invoked against us. It is a bit more challenging to look inwardly at ourselves and request forgiveness for the laundry list of wrongs that we have inflicted on others, consciously or unconsciously. Say a prayer before you begin and prepare yourself for the raw emotions to follow. If the person you feel betrayed by is not available, or they are too toxic, then use a friend or loved one to stand in their place.

Be careful, this is not an exercise you should use to fall back into a less than ideal relationship, but an exercise to help free you to move forward.

Lessons learned:
- ➤ Be honest about the contributions you made to your own circumstances. (Ouch!)
- ➤ Seek forgiveness.
- ➤ Forgive. Forgive. Forgive.

NOTES

NOTES

CHAPTER 7
THIRD TIME'S A CHARM

"And now these three remain: faith, hope, and love. But the greatest of these is love."
1 Corinthians 13:13 (NIV)

While still at home assisting my family after my uncle's funeral, I received a phone call from my friend, Ray. He called to notify me that one of his friends, an old college roommate, had been injured in an automobile accident. He was referring the friend to my office for legal assistance. He also told me this was the same friend he had spoken to me about previously and he wanted to introduce us.

Ray said, "His name is Marshun Middleton. Look out for his call."

My curiosity was piqued. I said, "Okay."

I returned to Jacksonville later that week. On the

morning of Mr. Middleton's appointment, I also had a couple of court hearings. While in court, my secretary notified me that he had arrived for his appointment. As he completed his intake questionnaire, I was wrapping up my hearings. I was anxious to meet this new client who awaited me. When I returned to the office, he was prepared for our consultation.

I had to pass him in the conference room to get to my office to put my briefcase away. I greeted him and advised him I would be right with him. He was very easy on the eyes. I immediately did a mental check on my appearance. Were my hair, makeup, and clothes in order? Because his appearance certainly was. In my office, I checked myself out in the mirror. I had on one of my cutest skirt suits. The skirt was black and landed right above my knees. The jacket was black and white, and I wore a black, spaghetti-strap tank top underneath. I wore a pair of medium-height, black, chunky-heeled shoes. My hair and makeup were on point. Yeah, I was ready.

A few minutes later, I put my jacket back on and went up front to escort him to my office. I perused the front page of his intake forms that contained all the pertinent information that I was interested in. Marital status? Single. Children? None. Highest education level completed? Master's Degree. Religion? Methodist. Occupation? Football coach and educator. Inward smile. Promising start.

After silently browsing through the intake forms, I proceeded with the consultation. We briefly discussed the motor vehicle accident that had brought him to my office. Then our conversation turned to football. At the time, he was coaching football at a local college. He had also played football at Tennessee State University with Ray. I told him about my love of football and asked him what position he'd played in college. He said, "Center."

I nodded in understanding. He then asked, "You know, the person that brings the ball down the court?" I laughed.

He was testing me. I informed him that I was aware of the difference between the center in football and the point guard in basketball. Sense of humor? Check. We talked more about football. I understood the basics, but I really wanted a deeper understanding. He took a sheet of paper and started drawing out plays and explaining the purpose of each position on both offense and defense. I was immediately drawn to him.

At the conclusion of the consultation, I asked him to return to my office at his convenience with the photographs of the property damage on his vehicle, since he'd left them at work. The college where he worked was five minutes from my former office. He said he would return with the photos. He was back within the hour. I hadn't expected him to return so quickly. I had a lunch appointment with a former male co-worker, which had been scheduled for immediately after my appointment with Mr. Middleton. He returned to the office with the photos around the same time I was leaving the office with my lunch date. I cringed. I immediately wanted to explain to him that Joe was just a friend. I needed him to know that I was available. He told me later that he has never been the jealous type, but that day, he was.

After work, on the drive home, I could not stop thinking about Mr. Middleton. I found myself blushing. I called my bestie and told her all about him.

At the conclusion of all appointments, our clients were given a folder with information about our office and what to expect during the course of their case. The packet also included a short bio of the attorneys. My new client later admitted that after leaving the office, he thoroughly read through my bio. The next day, he called me with questions about my background. I blushed. *Does this mean he's interested?*

We talked for a while. He asked if he could take me out to dinner sometime.

"I would love that," I said. *I guess he is interested,* I told myself.

I wasn't sure it was a smart idea to date a client while

the case was pending. I also wasn't sure it was ethically allowed by the Bar. Not wanting to violate any rules, I called the Bar and inquired. I was pleased to learn that I would not violate any ethical rules as long as I wasn't exchanging sexual favors for legal services. That certainly was not going to be a problem. But I thought I had better take it a step further and run it by my boss. I informed him I had already taken the initiative and contacted the Bar. My boss said, "In my opinion, it's not a wise idea to date a client until the case is concluded."

My heart dropped. I had no idea how long it would be before his case concluded. Cases can resolve within months or, in some cases, it could take years. I was certainly not going to wait years to go out on a date, nor did I want to wait months. I enjoyed conversations with him, he made me laugh, and did I mention that he was easy on the eyes?

Therefore, I did what any clever young attorney would do. I analyzed that conversation with my boss without clarifying. It seemed to me he'd said he didn't think it was a wise idea but not that he was forbidding it. Yep, I had the green light to proceed with caution.

A short time later, we met for lunch. At lunch, I found myself pouring my heart out. I wondered if I'd talked too much. He seemed to be interested. It was a lovely lunch. I had to remind myself to take it slow. Lunch was followed by numerous long phone conversations.

We met up another evening at the beach and went for a walk, one of my favorite pastimes. He was so easy to share with, and I was so attracted to him that it was scary. We walked hand-in-hand. His touch sent tingles up and down my spine. Be still, my beating heart. He told me, during the writing of this book, that he'd fallen in love with me that night.

On a later occasion, we attended the same networking mixer. We decided to sit in his car and talk. While sitting in his car, at some point during the conversation, he leaned over to kiss me. Now if you've ever seen sparks fly and fireworks go off, like in the movies, that's exactly what happened with that first kiss. He was so sweet and gentle. Afterwards, he looked me in my eyes and said, "What was that? Did you feel that?"

Hallelujah! Yes, I did. I was happy I wasn't the only one who felt it. It was the most amazing connection I had ever felt. "Yes," I blushed.

At that point, we weren't completely dating. We were still being cautious and waiting on his case to conclude. (Ugh! I was trying my best to rush that case to resolution!) But because we were spending a little time together and appeared to be willing to explore a relationship, I wanted to share my past with him before he was in too deep and perhaps resented me for not telling him sooner.

One day I called him and shared everything regarding my two failed marriages, incidents during the marriages, and all else in between. I knew that this was a lot of information to pour on someone at once, but I didn't want either of us to waste our time. I had done my work and was ready to move forward, one way or the other. My past was just that. I couldn't hide from it, nor would it have been fair to him. Accordingly, I spilled my guts.

He told me he needed a few days to process all that information. He honestly wasn't sure if he was willing to continue in the developing relationship. I was crushed, but I understood. I told him I would give him the time he needed to sort through everything.

A couple of days later, he called and asked me to come by the school to see him. I wasn't sure what to expect. When he walked up to my vehicle, he didn't have the same gleam in his eyes that he'd once had. My heart sank. I knew his decision had been made before he uttered a word. He confirmed that he didn't think he could go forward. I told him I understood and thanked him for being honest.

That evening after work I went home and cried. I cried because my past was continuing to haunt me. I wanted to be upset with myself, with my exes, with God. I didn't want to go through this turmoil each time I met someone. I questioned whether sharing so much at once was the right thing to do. I decided that it was better to share early rather than later after deep feelings were involved. So, I got myself together and decided it was for the best. After all, I am who I am. I couldn't change my past. I was finally at peace with it.

I couldn't change my past. I was finally at peace with it.

A day or two later, he called. He said he couldn't stop thinking about me. He couldn't help thinking we had a connection that he couldn't explain. He understood my past and, despite it, he wanted to give us a chance. Oh, happy, happy, joy, joy! God was working things out as I processed through that test. When I eyed him, that look was back in his eyes. You know, the one that says *I am taken aback by you. You light my fire.* That look. The kiss was even more pleasurable. I cried happy tears.

Shortly after that, his case concluded rather quickly, and we were a bit more open. We went on dates and learned more about each other. I learned that he grew up in church, was attending a local church, and loved the Lord. He loved his family and went home to Tennessee to visit when he could.

On August 30, 2004, his maternal grandfather transitioned to be with the Lord. He was planning to make the 10- to 11-hour drive to Moscow, Tennessee, for the funeral. He invited me to ride with him to meet his family. It was my pleasure to be there to support him. We talked the entire drive. I don't know what we talked about; I just remember that it was a very pleasant drive with lots of communication. I met his mom, aunts, uncles, and cousins. It was a memorable trip for us. Though I wasn't certain about getting married again, I was certain I wanted to spend a lot more time with this guy.

In 2006, he accepted an offer to coach at Lane College in Jackson, Tennessee. We had been dating for three years. I wasn't certain what the future held for us. I was not in denial about the strain that distance can have on relationships. I was supportive of his career goals and fully supported his decision to move.

We stayed in touch and continued our relationship. We visited each other as often as we could. After I picked him up from the airport on one of his trips, I serenaded him with Jennifer Hudson's song, "Love You I Do." I was so excited to see him.

When we made it to my townhome, and after I finally stopped singing, he kissed me. He then dropped to one knee and asked, "LaFonda, will you marry me?" I knew he was the one. Without hesitation, I said, "Yes!"

It was a short engagement. We married on May 25,

2007. On our day of love, there were no doubts as I dressed and no swollen eyes or infections. I was calm and untroubled. It was a beautiful sunset wedding with the St. Johns River splashing in the background.

We honeymooned in Hawaii on a seven-night cruise. On day six of the cruise, we went on an excursion to Haleakalā National Park in Maui. The elevation at the summit top was 10,023 feet above sea level. When we made it to the top of the summit, I stopped to read the informational signage.

A few minutes later, after noticing he wasn't with me, I looked around and did not see him anywhere. I panicked. I searched and searched. The rental car we were driving was gone. My heart was beating 1,000 beats per minute. I was trying desperately to remain calm. Surely, he wouldn't leave me stranded at the summit top of Haleakalā National Park all the way in Maui, Hawaii.

After I adequately worked myself into hysteria, he returned several minutes later. I was so upset with him for leaving me. The fact that he thought it was okay to leave me at the top of the summit was unsettling. He said he had to use the restroom and could not find any restrooms at the top of the summit. He left to go find one. I asked him not to leave me again in a foreign place without letting me know where he was. I was in full panic mode.

He realized that I was afraid he was leaving me; my fear was deeper than the few minutes I was left alone while he went to the restroom. He looked at me and assured me he wasn't going anywhere; that he was not going to leave me; that he was with me forever. My heart softened and melted. Reassurance. I thank God that He showed my husband what I needed at that moment.

Sometimes, even today, situations will arise, and that fear of abandonment will rear its ugly head. I thank God that He shows me when it is that underlying fear of abandonment that is driving my behavior, so that my response can be altered. I thank God that He has blessed me with a husband who can spot when this is happening, as well. When he realizes what's going on, he just stops, looks at me, and asks me to come to him so he can hug me and reassure me he's not going anywhere. We're not perfect. We make mistakes. But we are perfect together.

Even after doing the work, I sometimes have challenges. The lessons from the past may come back; we have to learn not to let them drive us.

As I write these words, my husband and I are approaching our eleventh anniversary. Our union has produced two energetic, loving, sweet boys. My husband also reluctantly accepts my dog, Smoky. My dreams have come true except for the white picket fence, and we're working on that, but white is no longer the dream.

TOOLBOX OF HOPE
TOOL 7: Meditate

Psalm 46:10 calls on us to "Be still, and know that [God is] God." (NIV) To *be still* means to sit quietly, stop thinking, stop trying to figure out solutions, just sit still. That's meditation. Also, Philippians 4:8 states, "Finally, brethren, whatever is true, whatever things are noble, whatever things are just, whatever things are pure, whatever things are lovely, whatever things are of good repute, if there is any virtue and if there is anything praise-worthy, meditate on these things." (NKJV) Further, when Jesus went out into the wilderness for 40 days and 40 nights, He meditated and spent time with the Father.

If Jesus meditated, then it seems that's something we should do also. Meditation has not always been a part of my routine, and oftentimes it is the first thing I take out of my busy daily schedule; however, meditation is such an amazing habit. It allows us to clear our minds and really hear a Word from God. Sometimes, with life happening all around us, it is difficult to steal away and spend a quiet moment with God. It is important to take a moment when we are still, to simply listen and expect a Word from God.

My dear friend, Denise, unexpectedly lost her husband of 15 years in a drowning accident. I was in awe of her strength and will to live a happy and healthy life despite her devastating loss. On one of my visits with her in her office, shortly after her husband's transition, she explained to me that she was able to function because she spent a lot of time meditating. Sometimes it only took five or 10 minutes of meditation to get her mind focused again. Her experience with meditation reminded me of its many benefits, and I was convicted to re-incorporate it back into my daily routine.

If you are not familiar with meditation, or you don't think you can sit quietly for a long period of time, I suggest starting with three to five minutes of guided meditation per day. Once you are accustomed to meditating, you can slowly increase the duration of the meditation.

I am in no way an expert or teacher on the practice of meditating. I will share with you my practice. I prefer to sit straight up with my feet planted on the floor, back straight, eyes closed, and hands resting comfortably in my lap or by my side. I begin by taking three to five very deep breaths. With each breath I visualize myself breathing in God's peace and love and breathing out all the disharmony and turmoil. As you breathe with your eyes closed, consider the following:

Breathe in God's love, breathe out fear.

Breathe in God's peace, breathe out anxiety.

Breathe in God's grace, breathe out shame.

Breathe in God's mercy, breathe out unforgiveness.

As you breathe deeply, feel God's love surrounding you.

Allow Him to speak to you.

Guided meditations are popular and can be found through a Google or YouTube search. Search for one that best fits your needs and personality. Some that you may try are:

The Mindful Christian, which can be found on YouTube.

Mindfulness, which can be found at www.mindfulworship.com.

Lessons learned:

- ➤ Always be honest.
- ➤ Trust the process.
- ➤ Don't allow pain and betrayal from the past to interfere and rob you of a happy present and future.

NOTES

NOTES

CHAPTER 8
A MESSAGE OF HOPE

*"May the God of hope fill you with all joy and
peace as you trust in Him, so that you may overflow
with hope by the power of the Holy Spirit."*
Romans 15:13 (NIV)

After each divorce, I went through the normal stages of grief
— denial, depression, anger, forgiveness, and finally,
acceptance. But I added to my stages a period of blaming God
for my poor choices, especially after the second divorce. I
accused Him of forsaking me. I accused Him of not protecting
me. I accused Him of leaving me. I begged and even
demanded answers from God.

I knew I was being ridiculous, but I honestly felt like God
had left me. He'd let me down. I was disappointed in Him.
Remembering my attitude toward God reminds me of an
incident that occurred recently with my five-year-old, Jordan.

One Sunday, my husband and I decided to drive separate cars to church because we had different obligations after the service. I told my boys what time I would be leaving and that if they wanted to ride with me, they should be prepared to leave at that time. I needed to leave a little earlier because I had to serve as a greeter. When the time came for me to leave, my eldest, Cameron, was ready and jumped in the vehicle with me. Jordan was not prepared to leave. Cameron and I left. Before we made it to the entrance of our neighborhood, my phone rang. It was my husband asking why I'd left Jordan.

I heard Jordan in the background crying uncontrollably because I'd left him. My heart broke - and I'm a sucker - so I turned around to go get him. When he got in the car, his face was tear-stained. After he calmed down, I thought it was a perfect opportunity to speak to him.

"Jordan, when you woke up this morning I informed you and your brother that I would be leaving at 8:45. I also told you if you weren't ready by that time that you could ride with your dad and I would see you at church." I tried to make eye contact with him through my rearview mirror. He was so upset he wouldn't even look at me.

"But I was almost ready!" he proclaimed.

I realized the underlying issue was that he thought I had abandoned him.

I softened my tone. "Jordan, the one thing that you can count on for sure is that, as long as I'm alive, I will never leave you for good. I was only going to church and I knew you were coming with your dad. I will always be there for you when you need me."

He was somewhat satisfied but still visibly upset that I'd had the audacity to leave him.

A couple of weeks after that incident, I asked the boys to take their baths while I prepared dinner. Jordan was to take a bath in the master bathroom and Cameron in their bathroom. I went back to our bathroom to check on Jordan while at the same time preparing dinner.

When I entered the room, I didn't see him. I called his name several times, and he didn't answer. I knew he was in there, but I was not in the mood, nor did I have time to play games with him. I told him that I knew he was in there, and I needed him to go ahead and take his bath. I left the room and went back to the kitchen to finish preparing dinner.

A minute or so later, he came running out of the bedroom, face drenched with tears, crying uncontrollably. I could barely understand what he was saying. I asked him to stop and take a breath. When he was finally able to speak, he angrily blurted out, "You said you would never leave me, but you did leave me!" I was confused. I thought he was referring to the incident a couple of weeks before. When I asked if that was what he was talking about, he said, "No! I was in your room! You didn't find me! You just left me."

I laughed. "But I was in the house with you," I said. I

realized he was upset that I'd left the room. It was so ridiculous that I had to try my hardest to keep it together, because I knew he was seriously hurt. I sat him down and explained to him that I had not left him. I gave him a hug and assured him that Mommy was his biggest champion and would always be in his corner.

When I think of my five-year-old and how hilarious I found that incident, I remember how angry I was with God and how ridiculous I must have sounded, as well. Of course, He didn't leave me. He has never left me. He was always there. He is my biggest fan and He's always rooting for me.

It's important to remember that, despite your circumstances, whether you are having a tough time in your marriage, going through a divorce, going through a break-up, already divorced, or whatever your circumstances may be, God is right there by your side. He is cheering you on. He's there to help you to lift yourself up, dust yourself off, and move forward. He promised in His Word that He will "never leave you, never forsake you" (Heb. 13:5, NIV).

> *He promised in His Word that He will "never leave you, never forsake you" (Heb. 13:5, NIV).*

Pastor Russ of Southpoint Community Church said in one of his sermons (and I paraphrase here):

Imagine that God is right there by your bedside when you wake up in the morning, bent over at the waist, hands on His knees so He is face-to-face with you, smiling, and cheering you on. He's saying, 'Good morning. I've been waiting on you. Come on, get up. Let's do this together.' My God, what a vision. In fact, God is there when you sleep, there when you awaken, there with you throughout your day. Just look at Him, acknowledge Him and let Him fight your battles. Together with God, you can.

There is hope on the other side. You must do your work, give God complete control, and look forward to brighter days ahead. Like the Father, I believe in you. I pray for your peace and happiness.

TOOLBOX OF HOPE
TOOL 8: Ministry through Song

David said in Psalm 69:30 (NIV), "I will praise God's name in song and glorify Him with thanksgiving." Just like David, we should find worship songs that speak to our heart and glorify and worship God despite our brokenness.

While going through heartaches, music ministered to my soul. Music can transform my mind, my spirit, and my emotions. It is soothing and healing to the soul. I would listen while driving to work, while sitting at home alone, while in the shower. Find a few songs that can really minister to you, and when you are feeling blue, listen to your song at high volume and dance, dance, dance.

Just a few of my favorites are:

➢ "Turning Around for Me" by Vashawn Mitchell
➢ "You Are the Living Word" by Fred Hammond
➢ "In the Eye of the Storm" by Ryan Stevenson
➢ "Worth" by Anthony Brown and group therAPy
➢ "Never Would Have Made It" by Marvin Sapp
➢ "Worthy of It All & I Exalt Thee" by Kalley Heiligenthal
➢ "Overcomer" by Mandisa
➢ "While I'm Waiting" by John Waller
➢ "Oceans (Where Feet May Fail)" by Hillsong

> "I Surrender" by Hillsong

I have spent many days riding in my car with the volume turned up, singing and crying. I've spent many nights in my home with the music blasting while singing, dancing, and releasing. Praise and worship Him, and He will take care of you in the process.

Second Corinthians 4:8-9 (NIV) states, "We are hard pressed on every side, but not crushed; perplexed, but not in despair; persecuted, but not abandoned; struck down, but not destroyed." You are not crushed, not abandoned, not destroyed. Rise up and live.

Lessons learned:
> You have never been abandoned.
> Never lose hope.
> Rise up and live!

NOTES

NOTES

NOTES

ABOUT THE AUTHOR

LaFonda Middleton was married and divorced times two before she reached the age of thirty. Her goal is to encourage and give hope and tools to ladies and young girls who have been broken due to broken relationships.

LaFonda is an attorney licensed in Florida, Georgia, and Tennessee. She is the sole owner and operator of The Middleton Law Firm, where she practices personal injury law.

She is married to Marshun Middleton and their union has produced two energetic young boys, Cameron and Jordan. They, along with their dog Smoky, reside in Jacksonville, Florida.

For speaking engagements, book club discussions, or retreats, LaFonda can be reached at lafonda_middleton@aol.com or on Facebook @LaFonda Gipson-Middleton.

Made in the USA
Columbia, SC
10 May 2024

35508706R00089